THE BAFFLED PARENT'S GUIDE TO

COACHING YOUTH
BASEBALL

Look for these other Baffled Parent's Guides by Ragged Mountain Press

Great Baseball Drills: The Baffled Parent's Guide,
by Jim Garland

Coaching Youth Basketball: The Baffled Parent's Guide,
by David G. Faucher

Great Basketball Drills: The Baffled Parent's Guide,
by Jim Garland

Teaching Kids Golf: The Baffled Parent's Guide,
by Detty Moore

Coaching Boys' Lacrosse: The Baffled Parent's Guide,
by Greg Murrell and Jim Garland

Coaching Youth Soccer: The Baffled Parent's Guide,
by Bobby Clark

Great Soccer Drills: The Baffled Parent's Guide,
by Tom Fleck and Ron Quinn

Coaching Youth Softball: The Baffled Parent's Guide,
by Jacquie Joseph

THE BAFFLED PARENT'S GUIDE TO
COACHING YOUTH
BASEBALL

Bill Thurston

Head Coach, Amherst College

With Tim Loescher, Nomad Communications
Norwich, Vermont

Ragged Mountain Press/McGraw-Hill

Camden, Maine • New York • Chicago • San Francisco
Lisbon • London • Madrid • Mexico City • Milan • Montreal
New Delhi • San Juan • Seoul • Singapore • Sydney • Toronto

I dedicate this book to young players, their parents and youth coaches who want to learn and teach the game of baseball. As a young player, I was very fortunate to have had coaches and knowledgeable baseball men who not only taught proper baseball fundamentals and techniques, but who also instilled in us a love and respect for the game. May the readers of this book better understand the challenges of coaching and teaching and enjoy the excitement, pleasure, and satisfaction that the game can bring players, coaches, and fans.

Ragged Mountain Press

*A Division of The **McGraw-Hill** Companies*

10 9 8 7 6 5 4 3

Library of Congress Cataloging-in-Publication Data
Thurston, Bill.
    The baffled parent's guide to coaching youth baseball / Bill Thurston.
        p.   cm.
    Includes index.
    ISBN 0-07-135822-6
    1. Youth league baseball—Coaching. 2. Baseball for children—Training. I. Title.
    GV880.65.T58   2000
    796.357'62—dc21   99-089655

Questions regarding the content of this book should be addressed to
Ragged Mountain Press
P.O. Box 220
Camden, ME 04843
http://www.raggedmountainpress.com

Questions regarding the ordering of this book should be addressed to
The McGraw-Hill Companies
Customer Service Department
P.O. Box 547
Blacklick, OH 43004
Retail customers: 1-800-262-4729
Bookstores: 1-800-722-4726

This book is printed on 70-lb. Citation
Printed by Quebecor Printing, Fairfield, PA
Design by Carol Gillette
Photographs pages 10, 11, 21 by Tom McNeill. All other photographs by Mark Washburn
Production management by Dan Kirchoff
Edited by Tom McCarthy and Jane M. Curran

Incredi-balls is a registered trademark.

Contents

Part One

Coaching 101: The Coach's Start-Up Kit

Part Two

Drills: The Foundation for Development, Success, Happiness, and a Coach's Peace of Mind

Introduction: So You Said You'd Be the Coach, Huh?

You'd heard that John Grisham, in addition to writing best-selling novels, is a proud Little League baseball coach in Charlottesville, Virginia, and you thought it sounded like fun. So when your daughter's league needed a coach, you decided to give it a shot. But now the realization of what you have opted into has hit home. You have never coached anything in your life, and, in fact, you haven't even played since *you* were in middle school. Nevertheless, in a few short weeks 15 youngsters and their parents are going to expect you to navigate them through a rewarding and fun experience in the National Pastime. Feel any pressure?

Don't worry. There's been a call placed to the bullpen and relief is at hand!

This book is designed to help you, regardless of your background in the game of baseball, navigate your way to a successful season. And by *successful* I don't mean more wins than losses. Success is determined by your young players learning teamwork and sportsmanship, developing basic baseball skills, and, most importantly, having fun. Whether you're coaching a team of fourth graders or want to work one-on-one with your own son or daughter, this book is designed to provide detailed instruction for individualized skill development. All the drills can be adapted for use by only one or two players and can be practiced in a backyard, vacant lot, or anywhere you have a little room to move and no windows to worry about breaking.

The advice and drills in this book are aimed at coaching 6- to 12-year-old players. They're kids who might be facing a pitched ball for the first time and kids who have done that for 6 years. These players represent a lot of fun and a great deal of challenge. Some will know more about the game than you, whereas others will need help putting on their gloves. Some kids will be making diving catches while others will be afraid of the ball. And some will be aggressive and enthusiastic while others will prefer watching the action. All your players, however, want to enjoy their time on the team, can experience the thrill of individual development, and can learn from you. These, and many others, are challenges we deal with throughout the book.

How to Use This Book

Coaching Youth Baseball: The Baffled Parent's Guide is like an organized assistant, providing advice on everything from the philosophy of the game to the logistical hurdles necessary to get the season going. It also contains a system of individual technique and skill development, from the basics to more advanced skills, complete with a grab bag of drills and clear illustrations to guide you. Though the book takes you through the season in a logical way, it is best used in segments as a reference to specific needs and issues.

Part One, Coaching 101: The Coach's Start-Up Kit, will introduce you to the game and take you through the beginning of the season. If you want advice on how to establish yourself as the coach and the authority in a positive and encouraging manner and how to create an environment that commands respect as well as the proper way to field a ground ball—then read chapter 1, Creating an Atmosphere of Good Habits. If you need to understand the basics of the game, from how many outs there are in an inning (what's an inning, anyhow?) to the positioning of your shortstop, read chapter 2, Before Hitting the Field: Baseball in a Nutshell. If you need a checklist of all the things that need to be done in preparation for the first day and strategies for how to do them, read chapter 3, Setting Up the Season. To learn all about the fundamentals of playing and coaching baseball, turn to chapter 4, Essential Skills—and How to Teach Them. To find help designing practices, assigning positions, and developing your players, read chapter 5, The Practice, and chapter 6, Sample Practices. For how to deal with game day and, specifically, answers to such questions as "When do I bring in a relief pitcher?", "How do I arrange a pattern of substitution?", and "How do I keep score?", read chapter 7, Game Time. And if you need help assessing the season or dealing with the many parent and gender issues that arise within a season, read chapter 8, Dealing with Parents and Gender Issues.

Part Two, Drills: The Foundation for Development, Success, Happiness, and a Coach's Peace of Mind, is what all coaches dream of—a reservoir of drills designed to address all facets of the game: batting, fielding, pitching, base running, team defense, you name it. First mentioned in chapter 4, these drills are illustrated in greater detail, designated as easy, intermediate, or advanced, and broken down into offense and defense. A great way to use this section is to try the drills as they are explained and then perhaps modify them according to the abilities of your players. I find that these drills have worked, but I am continually modifying them as I see fit. Just as no two 6-year-olds are the same, so are no two teams the same in personality and specific areas of strength and weakness. So feel free to make adjustments.

Drills are numbered consecutively by type, which we've broken into four areas: warm-up (W), defense fundamentals (D), batting practice (B), and ending activity (E). Drills are numbered consecutively by type (for example, W2 is warm-up drill 2, Running in Place) and are assigned a difficulty level. All drills are designated *easy* unless otherwise indicated. An easy drill is appropriate for a beginning player: there are no prerequisites. An *intermediate* drill assumes that the player has mastered elementary skills and has learned some basic baseball terminology. A drill labeled *advanced*—and there are few in this book—assumes the player has game experience and is familiar enough with the game to perform the technique or drill.

Throughout the book you'll also find helpful Questions and Answers sections that address common and hard-to-handle issues and sidebars designed to encourage you and to provide a little more information. Helpful photos demonstrating proper technique can be used as teaching tools. An appendix with Umpire Signals, a sample page from a scorebook, a glossary, and a resources section rounds out the information. A detailed index helps you find what you need when you need it.

A Word on Coaching

Be aware: this book is structured to assist you as the coach. Use it as a guide and reference. Every coach has his or her own personality *and* coaching style, but long-term successful coaches have many common traits. One good coach might be high on enthusiasm, and another might be calm and quiet. But remember, both can be good coaches. This book is a tool . . . if you use it effectively it will help prepare you for the experiences ahead.

Always remind yourself that your goal is to provide a fun and rewarding experience for your team. Continue to stress good habits and encourage your players to be receptive to learning. Emphasize strong effort, and stress and emulate courtesy and respect for one another, your opponents, umpires, and for the game itself. As your players' coach and leader, you are also their teacher and mentor. By what you say and especially by what you do, you can teach them the importance of teamwork, personal behavior, and responsibility, as well as the development of baseball skills. You have the opportunity for teaching the value of competition, that winning and losing are both part of the positive experience, and that having fun and developing skills is the name of the game.

Proper equipment and safe playing facilities are a must for a good learning experience.

Teach your players how to organize and take proper care of their equipment.

With or without coaching credentials, Grisham or not, you have the responsibility and capability of teaching your players lessons about baseball and lessons about life. You and they have the opportunity to make a positive impression and to enjoy a rewarding experience.

Here are five keys to being a good coach; they'll help you keep everyone involved, alert, and active.

Remember the Scouting motto: always be prepared. Every time you walk out onto the baseball diamond, have a plan for what you want to accomplish during practice that day. Know what drills and plays you'll work on and how long you want to spend on each one. Make sure that you are familiar enough with what you plan to do so that you can present it clearly. Plan on keeping everyone involved—active and alert. By organizing your thoughts and preparing a practice plan ahead of time, you'll keep the kids active, interested, and receptive to learning.

On the other hand, be flexible: if it isn't working, do something else. You don't have to be a psychiatrist to judge when kids are motivated and having fun, and when they are bored. You can have a great practice plan on paper, but if for some reason it's not going well, be ready to change your plan and move on to something else.

Good words go a long way: keep it positive. Everyone loves praise and encouragement. Make sure that one of your cardinal rules is that the coach is the only person *ever* to criticize a player—and then only in a positive, constructive way. Kids should never criticize other players. And remember that kids never can hear enough of "Great job," "Nice try," or "Good work." Positive encouragement is vital to a positive experience.

Keep your energy level high. You need to match the energy level of the kids you'll be coaching and to show excitement and enthusiasm about the game, every day, all the time. Psych yourself up before each practice so that you are excited and energized from the moment you step onto the diamond. Your players will feed off of your energy, and everyone will perform better because of it.

Keep your eyes open and get to know your team. One of the best ways to learn to coach your team effectively is to observe. Watch your players carefully; get to know their personalities. You'll learn a lot just by watching how they react and interact with each other. And be sure to learn every player's name right away—they need the recognition and will respond positively to it.

PART ONE

Coaching 101:
The Coach's Start-Up Kit

CHAPTER 1

Creating an Atmosphere of Good Habits

The Essentials

Discipline and organization are as important to a coach as they are to a parent or a teacher: a team needs a leader to direct the players and to get things done. Establishing this kind of control is essential to create an atmosphere of good habits and fun. Learning how to organize and control group behavior requires discipline played out through positive reinforcement and encouragement. This does not mean that you assume a dictatorial role, but rather, with organization and enthusiasm, teach kids to respond to your direction through fun activities. You'll be dealing with different personalities and skill levels—some kids who are excited to play, others who feel more comfortable in the background, and one or two who are wearing their gloves on the wrong hands—but you can offer each player the same encouragement and can reinforce positive team behavior. Kids prove again and again that positive energy is contagious and that doing what is expected of you is rewarding.

And that is just what good habits are: actions that need to be consistently reinforced and practiced. It's very important that you establish a routine that challenges your team and creates a situation where goals are clear and attainable. In the process of establishing routine and reinforcing good behavior, you'll confirm your role as the person in charge. Begin practice the same way every day: standing by the third-base line, you call "Bring it in!" and the kids come to you. That is how practice should happen every day of the season, with few variations. After your team has gathered, outline the day's practice: what drills you'll be doing and what skills you'll be learning and developing. The practice should end in the same way. After calling "Bring it in!" summarize what the players worked on and reinforce areas in which you've seen improvement. Take specific examples from practice and use the time to single out those who had a particularly good practice or who exhibited outstanding effort in a certain drill. Keep it positive and upbeat. Let the kids know when and where your next meeting will be and end with a team cheer.

Creating an atmosphere of good habits also includes the freedom to make mistakes. In addition to promoting good behavior, you're teaching them how to develop and improve as players. Those who attempt to do the right thing, even if they fail over and over, need to be encouraged and applauded for their efforts. Teach them not to fear failure—it's a part of the learning process. There's a tendency for kids to do what's comfortable and, consequently, to perpetuate bad habits that they've developed. For example, because kids lack the strength of older players, they often have an *uppercut* swing, which makes contact difficult and pop-ups frequent. The process to level out this uppercut is initially difficult, but correcting this swing is essential for a player to have any success as a hitter. So by encouraging "athletic risk taking" for the sake of improvement, you'll be working toward an atmosphere where mistakes are accepted but improving skills is the goal.

Competition

"Winning isn't everything, but trying to win is." I think that this little saying incorporates the essence of competition. Wins and losses are all part of competition, and development can be derived from either. The key is "trying to win," because it draws out the necessity to do things well, and doing things well requires hard work and practice. Without the goal of winning, the process of competition would lose many of its educational qualities. As often as I can, I like to create little competitive games within drills and throughout practice. This makes the drills fun and intense, exposes players to the need for execution under gamelike pressure, and facilitates concentration and teamwork.

Establish Your Identity as the Coach

Your players need to know what to call you—you're going to have your own children, your friends' children, and kids you don't know on your team. Whatever you decide you want to be called—"Coach," your first name, or a nickname—make sure that you keep it consistent. During practice or game hours, everyone must call you by this name—players, friends, parents, whoever. This way everyone will feel that they have been treated with the same respect and encouragement.

Helping Your Players Become Good Sports

There is a fine line between winning and losing. It often comes down to proper preparation, attention to details, and a confident, positive attitude. Young players need to play the game enough to feel comfortable in various game situations, to experience satisfaction, and to learn how to compete. Success breeds confidence, and the pride of being a good player drives youngsters to compete and work at the game.

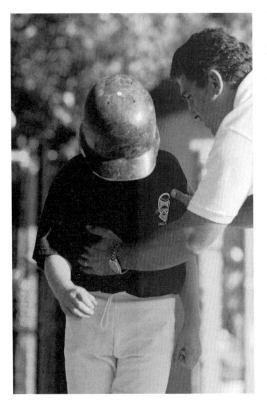

Another word for *coaching* is *teaching*. Be supportive of your players' efforts.

The Growth Book

A great way to develop your players is to keep a notebook in which you record each player's progress in certain areas. As early in the season as possible, jot down their strengths and weaknesses as players. For example, you may observe that, relative to her teammates, one player makes consistent contact in the soft-toss hitting drill but has trouble making contact with a pitched ball. You should also comment on the players' attitudes in practices and at games. Focus on the positive, but be honest with your players. For example, you might point out a player's steadfast perseverance in learning new drills and willingness to encourage teammates after a mistake but note that he needs to exhibit more self-control by displaying the utmost respect for the umpires and the job that they do. Continue to hone your notes in the growth book as you come to a better understanding of each player's development and attitude.

The growth book accomplishes three major things. First, it represents an object of accountability. Your players will want to improve and have that improvement noted in the book. Second, it identifies specific areas for each player to work on and establishes concrete goals. For instance, if a player is having difficulty bunting, you can reinforce her attention on this skill. Challenge her to execute more successful bunts out of 10 attempts each week and record the results of the drill. This allows you to focus your encouragement of her and creates a sense of growth and accomplishment for the player. Third, by pointing out the strengths of a player to the individual and to the team, you build her confidence and self-esteem, and she will work on that skill *even more* because of the sense of pride that she wants to uphold.

Let Your Signal Be Their Guide

At the beginning of the very first day of practice, stand just outside the third-base line and call "Bring it in!" The kids, who'll be throwing and catching with one another or looking for bats and gloves, will straggle in one by one without much hustle or enthusiasm. After they all finally gather, let them know that when you call the team together, you expect an immediate response of sprinting to you. But tell them that they get another try. Send them back to where they were and to what they were doing before you called them. Call "Bring it in!" again. If they do not respond in the way you've explained, do it again until every player comes to the circle immediately. When the team gets it right, reinforce that with enthusiasm. Let them know that they're working like a team and have them acknowledge it, too, by giving three slaps into their gloves.

On Risk Taking

The key to satisfaction as a ballplayer is improvement, and the key to improvement is being willing to fail. Kids are often reluctant to risk failure, particularly in front of their friends. But in many of the game drills outlined in chapters 9 through 12, the rewards go to those players who do not fear failure. For example, in the Knockout drill (see drill D7 on page 127), players are rewarded for aggressively charging ground balls as opposed to backing up and waiting for the ball to come to them. Being aggressive may be new for young players and will result in many bobbled balls, but make it clear to them that getting an out and "staying with it" are dependent on being aggressive on the ball, not just lying back and fielding the ball cleanly.

Make taking a risk the objective of various games and drills as opposed to perfect execution. The benefits and the lessons about life that players will learn from this approach will be significant for years to come.

Questions and Answers

Q. I have a player on my team who is there only because her parents have forced her to play. She is constantly talking while I'm talking and is quite disrespectful. What do I do?

A. You will notice in this book that practice time is active and leaves little room for standing around. Keeping the kids moving and reinforcing positive behavior is a dynamite way of eliciting good effort and creating a fun environment. But when one person is distracting the rest of the team from this kind of positive focus, the issue must be immediately addressed. Use the four-strikes-and-you're-out policy, and maintain the emphasis of positive encouragement. For example, if a player is talking while you're explaining a drill, don't single her out. Instead, remind all the team members that they need to focus their attention on the task at hand, including listening to you when you are talking. If you get this player to respond, really reinforce that positive team behavior. If she still doesn't respond, then single her out. Quickly let her know that she is disobeying the team rule and you as the leader, and that she is not participating as a team member. If the behavior still persists, give her the choice to participate or not—make it her choice, not yours. Finally, if nothing else works, make her sit out. But don't leave her there. Suggest she join the group and repeat to her that the former behavior must not persist. If this works with her, great. It's over. But if the behavior reemerges or you find her sulking, remove her from practice and let her know that you and she need to meet with her parents to figure out a solution. The key is to address the problem immediately and to remember that it is not only acceptable but also helpful, both to the person and the parents, to demand respect for others in a positive and consistent way.

Q. I have a player who is consistently late to practice, but it's not his fault. His parents are late in bringing him. How do I deal with this situation?

A. Part of the privilege of playing on a team is respecting one's teammates and the rules that the coach has established. And as the coach, you need to enforce all the rules consistently and fairly. At the beginning of the season, explain both in person and in a note sent home to the parents your policies regarding lateness and absence without an excuse and asking your players to please call if they will be late or unable to attend. Explain in that note what the penalties will be if players violate these rules, such as having to wait on the bench until you invite them into practice, or having to sit out a game. Don't make exceptions for any one kid. Contact the parents as soon as possible and discuss various solutions, including the possibility of carpooling. Be consistent, and the majority of the team and parents will appreciate you for it.

Q. As the season has progressed, my team takes longer and longer to gather together at the start of practice when I call "Bring it in!" I now need to yell at them in an angry tone to get a response. How do I regain control?

A. Go back to the beginning. Call them in and reinforce to them the importance of their listening to you. If they continue to give you trouble, send them out again and try it again until they get it right. Do not begin practice until you are satisfied with their response to your call. You are the leader and the one responsible for teaching and enforcing good habits and proper behavior. Finally, when they do get it, reinforce their efforts with genuine positive reinforcement. Begin practice and, unless the problem arises again, leave the situation behind you.

Q. The disparity in ability on my team has lead to the better kids picking on less talented kids out of frustration. I can understand their frustration, but it is ruining the team atmosphere. What should I do?

A. Being a part of a team leaves no room for disrespect or intolerance of others' abilities. A team must function as a unit to experience fun and success. You need to clear the polluted atmosphere pronto! Bring the team together and discuss the situation. Ask one of the more talented players, "If you strike out, do you feel better if [a teammate's name] tells you 'That's all right,' or if she criticizes you for not getting a hit? And do you think that you would do better the next time if your teammates were encouraging you to get a hit, or if they were yelling at you, 'Don't strike out again'?" Your players will always opt for support, so reinforce to them that this is why the *rule* on your team is to encourage and respect, and never to put someone down. Tell them that for the rest of practice, the team will be practicing encouragement. Have them focus on building each other up throughout the various drills and activities. At the end of practice, find out from them how being encouraged made them feel and how it affected their performance. Keep the lesson positive and the atmosphere light, but reestablish the importance of what they have learned.

CHAPTER 2

Before Hitting the Field: Baseball in a Nutshell

Baseball is a game of quick bursts and periods of waiting, but in those waiting periods there's a lot to think about. And for the coach, there's hardly enough time to think about all that you should in between the action. This chapter is an overview designed to introduce you to the basics of baseball, including important rules, positioning, and even what to think about in between pitches. More specific advice and strategy will come in later chapters, but this should get you started in the right direction.

Basic Rules and Positioning

Baseball is unique in that it's the only sport where the defense has the ball. Specifically, there are nine players playing on defense at any one time in the following positions.

Infield

Pitcher: positioned on the pitcher's mound in the middle of the infield.
Catcher: crouches behind home plate.
First Baseman: positioned a few steps from first base.
Second Baseman: positioned between first and second base, but closer to second.
Shortstop: positioned between second and third base, but closer to second.
Third Baseman: positioned a few steps from third base.

Outfield

Left Field: positioned in the outfield so that the player views the batter between the shortstop and third baseman (distance away from home plate for all outfielders depends on the potential power of the batter and thus will vary).
Center Field: positioned in the outfield behind second base.
Right Field: positioned such that the player views the batter between the first and second basemen.

The Field Itself

Most fields will vary in their outfield dimensions; some will have fences and some will not. But what do not change are the distances between the bases and between the pitching rubber and home plate. The distance between the bases on a youth league field is 60 feet, and the distance between the rubber and home plate is 45 feet.

Innings and the Object of the Game

Games for older players last nine innings, but in most leagues for 6- to 12-year-olds they play only six innings. An inning begins with the "top" half and ends with the "bottom" half. The visiting or "away" team bats in the top half of the inning, and the "home" team bats in the bottom half. The object of the game is to score more runs than the other team, and runs can only be scored when your team is at bat. Runs are scored by touching home plate after safely advancing around all three bases. Defensively, the goal is to keep your opponent from scoring runs. A half inning changes from the top to the bottom after the defense has gotten three outs.

The Start of an Inning

As the pitcher warms up his arm by throwing to the catcher, the first baseman can warm up the other infielders by throwing ground balls to them while the outfielders throw fly balls back and forth. When the pitcher feels loose and ready, the umpire signals play, and the pitcher throws to the batter in an attempt to get him out, the game is underway.

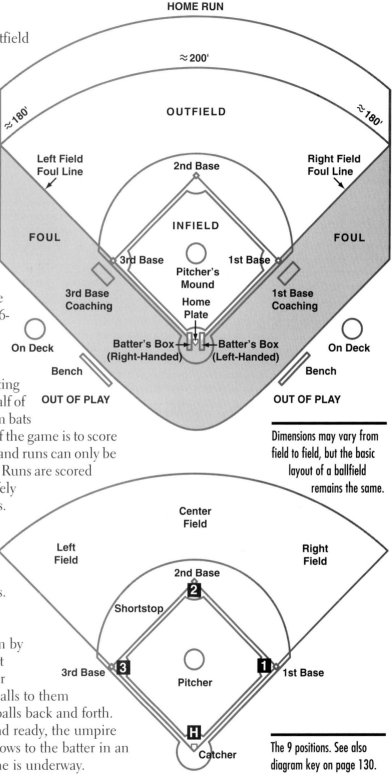

Dimensions may vary from field to field, but the basic layout of a ballfield remains the same.

The 9 positions. See also diagram key on page 130.

The Strike Zone and the Count

The strike zone varies for each batter, depending on the batter's size. The zone is as wide as home plate (17 inches) and extends vertically from the bottom of the batter's kneecaps to under the armpits. If the batter swings at the pitch and misses, it is automatically called a *strike*. If the batter does not swing, and the pitch is thrown outside of the strike zone, it is called a *ball*. If the batter does not swing, and the pitch does cross through the zone, it is called a *strike*. These calls are dependent on the judgment of the umpire—he "calls 'em as he sees 'em." Each batter receives a *count* of the number of balls and strikes. If the pitcher throws four balls it is called a *base on balls* or a *walk*. If the pitcher throws three strikes, the batter is out. If the batter hits a *foul ball*, which means a hit that does not land within the foul lines, it is considered a strike (unless there are already two strikes, in which case it does not affect the count). If a foul ball is caught in the air by one of the players on the field, the batter is out. A ball hit between the foul lines is a *fair ball* and must be fielded by the defense.

The Ball Is in Play

A batted ball can result in either the batter reaching base safely or being called out.

How a Batter Makes an Out

In addition to striking out, a batter can make an out by either grounding out or flying out. A *ground out* refers to a batted ball that is fielded off of the ground by a player and thrown to a teammate who then tags the base before the runner reaches it. A *fly out* refers to a batted ball caught by a defensive player before it touches the ground.

The strike zone. Left: The rule book strike zone (knees to the armpit). Right: Any part of the ball thrown over any part of the plate is a strike.

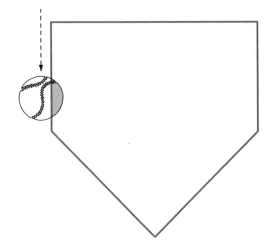

How a Batter Reaches Base

If the batter avoids making an out, she can reach base in a variety of ways. One way is the base on balls. A batter is also awarded first base if she is hit by a pitch. Once the ball is hit, the batter can reach base with a single, double, triple, or home run—all called *base hits*. She can also reach base on an error by a defensive player or by a *fielder's choice*, which means the defense chooses to get another base runner out while allowing the batter to reach base.

The Base Runner

Once a batter reaches base safely, he is considered to be a *base runner*. There are three basic rules that base runners must obey to avoid being called out. First, all base runners must occupy a base. Two players can never occupy the same base. Second, one base runner can never pass another on the base paths. And third, base runners can't advance on a fly out until the ball has been caught (this is called *tagging up*).

Once a player is on base, a variety of things can happen.

How a Base Runner Makes an Out

A base runner can be forced into an out by the defense tagging the base that the runner must reach before she actually reaches it. This is called a *force-out*. A defensive player who has the ball can tag a base runner who is not safely on a base. This is called a *tag out*.

How a Base Runner Advances around the Bases

A base runner can advance from base to base via a base hit, error, *passed ball* (a pitch that gets by the catcher), by *tagging up*, being forced (by a fielder's choice, base on balls, or the batter being hit by a pitch), or *stealing*. Stealing, at the youth-league level, is permitted when a base runner attempts to run to the next base just as the pitch crosses home plate. A base runner can steal second or third base, but in youth leagues stealing home is not an option.

Basics of Pitching

Pitchers throw from the pitcher's mound in the center of the diamond. They are required to have a foot touching the pitcher's *rubber*, which is a rubber rectangle fixed in the ground at the top of the mound. Young pitchers will often make the mistake of standing on top of the rubber, instead of placing their foot in front of the rubber for balance and weight transfer. This generates better power and balance as a pitcher.

As previously mentioned, the strike zone is dependent on the size of the batter and invokes the subjective judgment of the umpire. Sportsmanship, specifically respect for the umpires, is discussed several times throughout the book, but here it is appropriate to mention the impor-

A Sample Half Inning

There are countless possible scenarios that can take place in a given half inning, but there are plays and occurrences that are more common than others. The following section represents a sample half inning of play and includes a series of situations that your team is likely to encounter.

The first batter of the inning, after arriving at a comfortable stance in the batter's box, is ready to hit, and the umpire points at the pitcher as if to say, "Play ball!" The batter doesn't swing at the first pitch, but it's called a strike because it crossed the outside corner of the plate. The batter also lets the next pitch go by, but it's too high and is called a ball. On the third pitch, the batter swings and fouls the ball to the backstop, forcing the count to 1 and 2. The fourth pitch is out of the strike zone, but the batter swings and misses. Strike three is called, and the batter is out. One out, nobody on base, no runs scored.

The second batter is thrown two balls and, on the 2–0 count, hits a line-drive double down the right field line and into the corner. One out, runner on second base, no runs scored.

The third batter reaches a 0–1 count and then hits a ground ball that goes up the middle past the pitcher for a single. The runner who previously hit the double heads toward third base and is signaled by the third-base coach to try for home. The throw from the center fielder is thrown to the first baseman, who is acting as the relay person. There is no chance for the runner to be thrown out at home, so the catcher calls for the throw to be cut. This allows the first runner on base to score but keeps the runner who hit the ball from running to second base. One out, runner on first base, one run scored.

The fourth batter grounds a 3–1 pitch to the third baseman, who bobbles the ball and does not attempt a throw to first base. The batter reaches first base safely while the runner previously on first advances to second base. The play is ruled an error on the third baseman. One out, runners on first and second base, one run scored.

The fifth batter hits a fly ball to right field. The runner on first base positions herself halfway between first and second base so that if the ball is caught, she can return safely to first base, and if the ball is dropped, she can run to second base without being thrown out. The runner on second base tags up. The fly ball is caught by the right fielder, and the batter is out. As soon as the fly ball is caught by the right fielder, the runner on first base retreats to first while the runner on second tags up and runs to third base. The throw from right field is relayed by the second baseman to third base, but the throw is late and the runner is safe. Two outs, runners on first and third base, one run scored.

The sixth batter is thrown four balls and reaches first base on a walk. The runner previously on first base is then forced to go to second. Two outs, bases are loaded (runners on first, second, and third base), one run scored.

The seventh batter hits the first pitch to the shortstop, who tosses to the second baseman. The throw beats the runner coming from first and forces him into an out. Regardless of whether the runner on third base reaches home plate before the force-out is made, this runner doesn't score because the third out is a force-out. Final tally for the half inning: one run scored, two base hits, one error.

tance of the pitcher's attitude. The pitcher needs to be encouraged to maintain her composure and contain her emotions on the mound. Whether an error is made by a teammate or the umpire makes a questionable call, the pitcher must respect the effort and judgment of both. Sour expressions or argumentative words from the pitcher reflect poorly on you, on her parents, and on her—not to mention that it makes throwing the next pitch for a strike even more difficult. As a fun learning activity, sometime during the season have each pitcher serve as umpire during a scrimmage or a drill in practice. Each pitcher will gain respect for just how hard it is to call balls and strikes.

Your pitcher is the key for controlling the game. The most important skill is the ability to throw strikes.

The Batter's Box

On each side of home plate is a painted rectangle called the *batter's box*. The batter is required to stand within the box and should stand close enough to the plate that, when she swings, the barrel of the bat can reach the outside part of the strike zone. Young players have a tendency to stand too far from the plate for fear of being hit by the pitch. You need to encourage them to step up to the plate and be willing to swing aggressively.

The On-Deck Circle

The player waiting to hit next swings and warms up in the *on-deck circle*. This is often a dirt or painted circle located in foul territory and out of the way of the bench. Bats and helmets are kept near the circle, and players who are not "on deck" should stay on the bench.

Responsibilities of a Coach during the Game

Game coaching is covered in much greater detail in chapter 7, but here are the basics. As coach, you are responsible for assigning positions and making sure that you have nine players in their appropriate positions for each inning. Most importantly in this regard, you need to keep track of how many innings each pitcher has thrown the ball per week. Many youth leagues have a rule limiting the number of innings a pitcher can throw in a week (often six). If the league does not have such a rule, you ought to establish it as a team rule: each pitcher is limited to six innings per week.

When Your Pitcher Is in Trouble

A pitcher on the mound having trouble getting the ball over the plate is the loneliest player on the team. One of your roles as coach is to help your pitcher regain his concentration, focus, and confidence. Encourage your pitcher to think about the job at hand, not about what has already gone wrong. Try to help him make adjustments so he can work his way out of trouble. If the pitcher has completely lost his confidence or pitching rhythm, however, you should take him out of that situation and start him fresh another day.

In the Spotlight

No other sport highlights and records every detail, every individual play, like baseball. Probably even more than the memory of great games, people remember specific plays—both the heroic and the blundered. Who can forget Willie Mays's over-the-head catch in the Polo Grounds, Kirk Gibson's home run in the 1989 World Series, or Bill Buckner's boot in the 1986 World Series. The individual parts in a baseball game somehow become bigger than the whole picture, and for that reason, the individual player is cast into the spotlight. In a split second a player whose name has not been called all game is the one person who can make or break the game—and all eyes are fixed on her. Imagine your 10-year-old second baseman's reaction when she just watches a ground ball go through her legs with the tying runner on third base. The spotlight is on her. She knows she goofed, and if she is a young Red Sox fan, she probably can empathize in that moment with Buckner's pain. What she needs at that moment is encouragement and support, not criticism. Wait for the end of the inning, when your player is out of the spotlight, to tell her what caused her to commit that error.

You need to establish a substitution schedule for each game that allows equal playing time to all players who share positions (substitution is covered in more detail in chapter 7). While your team is at bat you are responsible for having first- and third-base coaches in their respective coach's box—located in foul territory beside their respective base. Though it is not required, I suggest that you be the third-base coach and that you create a rotating schedule of players who will be the first-base coach. This keeps the players who are not currently in the game still involved in the action. As third-base coach, you are responsible for calling specific plays and for directing the runners around the base paths.

Defensively you need to constantly be aware of your players' positioning, making sure that they are where they should be. Young infielders have a tendency to gravitate toward the bases while outfielders tend to migrate toward the foul lines. You need to keep an eye on them and make sure that they stay in their positions. You are also responsible for monitoring your pitcher's physical and mental condition on the field and for making pitching changes when the need arises. How to evaluate the condition of your pitcher and when to pull the plug on him for that day is described in more detail in chapter 7.

Basic Safety Measures

Baseball is a game played with swinging bats, hard balls, and fixed objects like backstops and fences. Common sense goes a long way in forming a safe playing environment; it can be a very dangerous game if you do not take necessary safety precautions. But if you are aware of the areas of potential danger and are diligent in creating and maintaining a safe practice environment, you can make the games and practices safer. As coach, you need to concentrate on the following areas of concern and learn how to avoid injury.

Helmets

Most of us would not allow our children to get on a bicycle without wearing a helmet, and the same thing stands true for baseball players on offense. Helmets must be worn by all players at bat and on the base paths. In addition, all base coaches, players rotating through the hitting drills outlined in chapter 6 (including those drills that don't include a ball), and players who are practicing their swings in the on-deck circle must wear a helmet. Any player who is on deck or preparing to swing a bat must check around him for other players, and team members need to be reminded to stay away from the on-deck circle if they aren't warming up to bat. If a player isn't in the game or in one of these "helmet situations," she must stay behind the fence. And perhaps most importantly, encourage your players to stay alert during the game. In a fun and positive manner, periodically quiz the players on the bench about the number of outs, the count of balls and strikes, what they would do if the ball were hit to them, and other points about the game. This not only promotes safety but also conditions the mental aspect of their development as players.

For safety's sake, and to learn by observing, kids on the bench should be taught to pay attention to what's happening on the field. Be part of the game!

The T-Ball Experience

T-ball is a gentle, nurturing introduction to baseball or softball. Played by 4- to 8-year-olds, the game is intentionally structured to expose kids to the basics without imposing too many rules. The t-ball veterans on your team will likely have a firmer grasp of fundamentals than your other players, but don't expect them to have *too* much of a lead on kids who haven't played at all.

In t-ball, the offensive team hits a ball off a waist-level tee. There's no intimidating pitcher and no fear of being hit by an errant pitch. This allows the ball to be put into play more easily, giving both offense and defense a chance to play.

Everyone plays in a t-ball game. There are no strikeouts, no walks, the field is smaller, and the offensive team is retired only when all its players have had a turn at bat, which leads to longer innings and sometimes astronomical scores. On defense, every player takes the field. If you've ever watched kids in action during a t-ball game, the first thing you'll note is that things are much looser, and total chaos is no stranger.

But that's just the point. Kids still learn to catch, throw, run the bases, and hit the ball. And most important, kids have fun as they learn the game.

Communication

Defensive players chasing after fly balls tend to have their heads up while they run. As a result, players can collide with other players or objects such as fences. For this reason, it is crucial that you teach your players to communicate and call for balls. Players who aren't in pursuit of the ball should let those that are know where the fence is. And if two players are in pursuit of the same fly ball, they need to communicate by calling, "I've got it" or "You take it." Drills for this are described in chapter 10.

Throwing

At the beginning of each practice and game, have your team assemble to warm up and throw the ball around, as in Five Every Five (see drill W15 on page 124 in chapter 9). It is crucial that you teach your players the proper and safe setup and execution of this drill. Players should always throw in the outfield and be perpendicular to one of the two outfield foul lines. Among the two partners, one player should be against a fence in foul territory while the other is in the field of play. After you yell, "Start!" they begin throwing. Players should never walk behind other throwers, they should always throw in the same direction (parallel to one another), and partners should make eye contact with one another before making a throw. If a throw is missed, the player jogs after the ball and then jogs back to the throwing position. He should *not* throw from where he picks up the ball. When you yell, "Hold the ball!" players should stop throwing immediately and follow your next instruction.

Batting

Players must stay clear of players who may be swinging bats, and a player planning to swing must check all around her to make sure that no one is in jeopardy of being hit. It is possible for bats to be released in the follow-through of a swing, and for this reason, players should never stand behind a batter. This includes batters at the plate as well as those who are hitting off of batting tees, hitting in a Soft Toss drill, or simply taking Dry Swings without a ball (see drill B5 on page 143 and drill B3 on page 142). The Tee-Hitting and Soft Toss drills (see drill B4 on page 142) also require a fence or a screen into which players hit baseballs. Make sure that the fence or screen has no pipes or cross-pieces that could cause the ball to carom and end up

The Discovery Method

One of the most effective ways of teaching children a skill is to use the *discovery method*—where they discover the answer for themselves. Here's how it works: you give them a demonstration of the technique you want them to do. For example, if you wanted to teach them how to catch a ball properly, instead of saying, "Trap the ball in the pocket of the glove," say: "Watch this. You tell me where the ball goes when I hold up my glove." Let your players tell you what is going on with the drill, and they'll find out themselves.

Honing the Basics

I grew up in a rural area where there were only four or five boys to play ball. For fun, we played catch, took batting practice, and fielded ground balls daily. If we didn't get 200 swings a day, it must have been raining. Today, young players do not do enough throwing (or hitting) to develop arm strength and arm stamina or to develop good baseball techniques through trial and error. Encourage your players to practice, practice, practice the basics of throwing and catching with each other—it's the best way to become good players.

hitting a player. Finally, train your kids to set down the bat after hitting the ball and before running to a base. Throwing the bat is a common problem among young players, and it puts both catchers and umpires in jeopardy.

Sliding

Despite the fact that kids see major leaguers slide headfirst into bases, youngsters should always go in feet first. The bent-leg slide described in chapter 4 is the only sliding technique that your players should use. Headfirst slides expose players' faces to spikes, baseballs, and sweeping gloves. The positioning of the shoulders in a headfirst slide can also result in serious injury. The bent-leg slide, on the other hand, keeps the head away from danger. It is also important that players not slide into first base except to avoid a tag or a collision. It is safer and, in fact, faster to simply run through the base.

Throwing Arms

Arm injury is a common problem from the youth leagues to the majors, and in most of these cases the primary causes are improper warm-up and overuse. Players need time to loosen up their arms at the beginning of practice and should slowly build up arm strength and stamina throughout the season. The Five Every Five drill (see drill W15 on page 124 in chapter 9) facilitates this progression. Pitchers are the most prone to arm trouble because of the problem of overuse. Don't allow pitchers to throw more than one game per week and restrict them to a maximum of 60 to 70 pitches per game (50 to 60 for players 10 and under). These are reasonable and safe limits to impose. Restricting pitchers, along with teaching them proper throwing mechanics (see chapter 4), will reduce the risk of arm injury.

Setting Up the Season

Most likely you are excited about the start of the season and are focusing in your mind upon the practices and games. But as CEO of your team, you must prepare both mentally and logistically for the season and for all the stuff that needs to get done before the first practice. This chapter will help you to do just that.

Create the Practice and Game Schedule and Send a Letter to Parents

Before any games of catch or even before a single pitch, you need to establish the practice and game schedule for the entire season. Plan on having three meetings per week, which often means two games and one practice. Fewer than three meetings can make it difficult to build on what your players have learned, and as a result, you wind up having to review more drills and concepts than you would have to otherwise. More than three meetings, however, can be a strain on a family's time commitments. Try to keep practices on the same days of the week and at the same times throughout

A Word on Tryouts

As a coach of a team of 8- to 12-year-olds, you're unlikely to face the prospect of formal tryouts, those often nerve-racking sessions in which a group of coaches evaluates potential players on such things as throwing, baserunning, hitting, and speed around the bases. As kids work their way into more competitive leagues when they're older, tryouts are necessary. But not now.

Tryouts have no place in a youth league at this level. Your league might bring kids together before the season to allow coaches to distribute experienced players equally, but this session should be no more than that. Your first priority is to teach baseball fundamentals and allow the kids to enjoy themselves. Your players might be fresh from T-ball, or they might have no experience at all. The drills and advice in this book are designed to allow you to work with everyone, regardless of their skill and experience.

Key to Success: Put That in Writing

Here are some issues that you may want to address in your letter to parents:

- Your coaching philosophy, including your attitude toward winning and losing, teamwork, and your overall objective of developing skills and having fun.

- Expectations for sportsmanship and behavior at practice and at games—for players, parents, and you.

- Goals for the season: what you want your players to get out of it, what you want to get out of it.

- Policies for tardiness, absence from games or practices, discipline issues.

---

the season. Finally, plan on distributing this schedule to the parents at the first practice.

Inevitably, however, there will be last-minute schedule changes as a result of weather or other complications. Thus, you also need to develop a telephone tree in order to contact families when changes occur (see a more detailed explanation of the phone tree on page 27).

Include with the schedule and phone tree a letter to the parents addressing your philosophy of coaching and your expectations regarding sportsmanship and commitment during the season (see the sample letter on page 26). It is important to be straightforward from the beginning regarding these issues. Your letter provides a clear reference point should an issue with a parent arise during the season. This letter will also hold you accountable to the same expectations.

Call the Parents before the Season

Once you have the names of all your players, take the time to call their parents and introduce yourself. Try to contact three to five parents per evening and keep track of those you reach and those for whom you leave messages. Briefly communicate your philosophy of coaching and your expectations, ask whether there is anything you should know concerning their child, and allow them time to respond and ask questions. This gives the parents an opportunity to share their thoughts and concerns in a private setting. Also during the call, let them know the time and place of the first practice and ask them to stay for the first 10 minutes for a brief meeting.

Solicit Parental Help

The first phone call is also an opportune time to ask the parents if they would be willing to help in any way throughout the season. Enthusiastic parents can help with carpooling and arranging rides to practices and away games, bringing water or wet towels to games, preparing snacks, phone tree responsibilities (including forming yours entirely), postgame treats or ice

Sample Preseason Letter to Parents

Dear Parents:

Another baseball season is upon us. I'm excited about our team and hope your kids are, too.

My primary goal for the season is for everyone to have fun and improve their baseball skills. My basic philosophy is to foster a positive, supportive atmosphere so that every player has a great experience. Regardless of ability, every member of the team deserves to be treated with encouragement. Players should respect each other on and off the field and should learn both to win and lose well. I look to you to help reinforce these important concepts: when you come to games or practices, please limit your interaction with your children to positive encouragement from a distance. During games, please treat the umpires with the respect they deserve. We are our children's most important role models. I'll set as good an example as I possibly can, and I would greatly appreciate your help by doing the same.

Games: Please make every effort to arrive at games 30 minutes before the scheduled start. If you know that getting your child to a game will be difficult, we can carpool. If your child can't make it to a game, please let me know in advance. If he or she misses practice the week before the game without a good reason, he or she might not play in the game. Please know that I have this policy so that participation in the games is fair for everyone.

Cancellation: Unless you hear otherwise, we'll always have practice or games. In the case of cancellation, kids will be notified either at school or by means of the enclosed phone tree.

Must Bring: Please make sure that your child has a water bottle, glove, and sneakers or rubber cleats. These, and other personal equipment, should be labeled with his or her name.

We're looking forward to a great season of baseball. If you have questions or concerns, please feel free to contact me.

Thanks,
The Coach
403 Lincoln Avenue
555-4007
coach@baseball.com

Calling All Volunteers!

If you have parents who want to be a part of the team but don't want to help out on the field, by all means use their enthusiasm to take over the administrative details. There are routine but important administrative aspects to running a team that could be taken over by a manager or several committed parents:

Phone Tree

Instead of having every kid call you whenever there's a threat of a shower or a change in the schedule, have one parent arrange a phone tree. You call one designated person, who then initiates a reliable chain of communication for the rest of the team.

Practice Transportation

A designated parent can be in charge of carpooling by checking that each player has a ride to practice and home again. Though many families won't need this help, the safety net that it provides for those who do is reassuring. This parent should make certain that all players are picked up from practice before he or she leaves.

Away-Game Transportation Schedule

It's a great idea to have a centrally located place where kids can meet before going to away games. A designated parent can schedule the time and place for meeting before away games and can make sure that there will be enough drivers to accommodate the players and that drivers have written directions to the ball park. Meeting like this before the game ensures that each player is accounted for and has a ride to the game, and it also builds team unity before the game.

Fund-Raisers

Getting all of the necessary equipment can be somewhat expensive. Having team dinners, organizing fund drives, and arranging other fund-raising events are projects that an administrative parent can organize, with some of the duties delegated to other team parents as well.

Snack Duties

A small, nutritious snack during practice or a trip to the ice cream stand after a game can be a helpful boost or well-deserved reward for your young players. A parent can be in charge of this service or can create a rotating schedule of parents who would be interested in helping. This is a fun and highly satisfying way that parents can become involved with the team.

cream, organizing equipment fund-raisers, and so on. Also, if you do not already have someone in mind for an assistant coach, you can ask if a parent would be willing to do it (see below for the assistant's responsibilities). A parent with administrative skills might be willing to serve as team manager. (See Calling All Volunteers!, above)

Finding an Assistant

The role of an assistant coach is extremely important, and even if it involves having a number of different volunteers coming on different days, you will be much better off with help from someone who is willing and enthusiastic. The assistant might be a high school player or another adult, but this is not the primary concern. Most importantly, your assistant must be someone who is committed to being the kind of enthusiastic role model for the kids

Set the Ground Rules with Your Assistant

Make sure that you explain your philosophy and expectations for behavior during the season, not only to your players and their parents, but to your assistants as well. You don't want to be out on the field with an assistant who doesn't share your philosophy of good sportsmanship, patience, or keeping things fun, and you need to make this clear before the season starts.

that you are trying to be. Distantly second to this main priority, it is helpful if your assistant can catch, throw, and hit.

Stress the fact that you're not asking for help in designing practices and the like, but instead you're looking for someone to step in and help with drills and teaching techniques. For example, in practice you will often need help hitting ground balls and fly balls and throwing for batting practice, and during games an assistant can help by gathering equipment and keeping the scorebook (see page 149 in the appendix). Even in the rare times when there is no direct assignment, a good assistant can give instruction, encourage, and supervise the players.

Appropriate Numbers of Players on the Team

The ideal number of players for a baseball team is 15, but if you have as few as 13 or as many as 17, you can still manage. It is probably rare, however, that you are blessed with just the number you would like. Having fewer than 15 might cause problems with fitting players in appropriate positions, though at young ages, this is not a major concern. Larger numbers of players can cause problems with playing time and individual attention. Breaking your numbers up into "teams" of infielders, outfielders, pitchers, and catchers can alleviate some of these problems, but with numbers too large, it becomes difficult to manage, even with an assistant.

Equipment

Baseball is an equipment-intensive sport. It's important to take an inventory of what's available and what you need to get. The first step in this process is to find out what can be provided by your recreation department. Whatever they can't provide, you can acquire through fund-raising events, parental donations, or a personal investment (equipment bought in bulk is considerably less expensive). Each player should be responsible for having his own glove, cleats, and water bottle. Sneakers can substitute for cleats, but metal spikes, it is important to note, are strictly illegal. Many players will have other personal equipment such as bats, batting gloves, and catching equipment in addition to items such as protective glasses. They must write their names and phone numbers on each piece of equipment so that everything is identifiable.

The equipment I list reflects the minimum amount necessary to effec-

Equipment Checklist

- Bats
- Baseballs
- Incredi-balls
- Helmets
- Catcher's gear
- Equipment bags (bat bag, helmet bag, ball bag, catcher's gear bag)

- Plastic cones
- First-aid kit and ice pack
- Whistle
- Clipboard, scorebook
- Team roster
- Growth book, telephone numbers for parents

tively work throughout a season. Having more bats or balls, for example, is a bonus and will be very helpful. Having less equipment will make things more difficult for effective practice sessions.

Bats

You'll need at least four aluminum bats of different lengths—to accommodate players of different size and strength—and none more than two years old. Bats that are older than this lose their explosiveness, their "pop," and often sting the hands. See the sidebar below for appropriate bat sizes depending on the age of the players. If a player has her own wooden bat, she can certainly use it. Kids often like the idea of having their own equipment, but unless the bat was purchased within the past year, chances are that the bat is not the appropriate size and that she would be better suited to using one of the team's bats.

It's vital that your players have a bat that they can handle. At the youth level, kids are not strong enough to swing a heavy bat.

Weighted Bat

A weighted bat is a great way to build strength and teach bat control for young hitters. But it's not a necessary piece of equipment. The other option is to buy a "donut"—no, not a cruller, but a traditional hole-in-the-center donut weight with a rubber coating that fits on to the barrel of the bat, making it heavier. Both create the same sensation when a player picks up a regular bat: "This thing feels light!"

Matching Bat to Batter

Most young players between the ages of 8 and 12 should use a 28-inch, 22-ounce bat. If you're not sure what size bats you have or if the bat is appropriate for the batter, watch your players swing. If they swing the bat and it dips as it goes around, the bat is too heavy. If the bat is level through the swing, it is probably the proper weight.

Baseballs

You will need at least 20 regular baseballs and 10 rubber or Incredi-balls for batting drills. You need to instill in your players an intense desire to never lose a ball, because otherwise it becomes very easy to lose 20 balls in a couple of practices. During batting practice, make it a game to retrieve the balls after each hitter, counting out each one as it comes in, timing how long it takes, and applauding those who find the greatest number. Even so, you may have to purchase baseballs several times throughout the season as you lose them or as they become waterlogged. You'll also need to purchase game balls.

Helmets

You will need helmets for a possible 8 players who would need helmets at one time: the batter, the runner on first base, the runner on second base, the runner on third base, the batter on deck, the player ready to go on deck, and the two base coaches. You'll need to have more than 8 helmets available, however, to make sure there are enough helmets in the right sizes (small, medium, and large). Your selection should cover all three sizes, though most of your players—depending on age, of course—will wear a medium.

Catcher's Gear

A batting helmet is essential for batters, runners, and base coaches.

Gear for catchers includes a catcher's mitt, chest protector, shin pads, a helmet and face mask, and and a protective cup for boys. Make sure to check that the helmet and face mask fit properly and don't easily slide upward or downward. If the equipment is used, check to see that all the straps and snaps are operable; if not, replace them. A new strap is a much better value than having to buy a whole new set of shin pads. If the opportunity arises to acquire a second set of catcher's gear, seize it. Having two sets allows you to perform more drills and to have more pitchers throwing at once during practice, not to mention the fact that it would allow you to have two different-sized catchers on your team!

Pitching and Protective Screens

Other pieces of equipment that might be available to you and that are very helpful, but not crucial, are pitching screens and protective screens at first base. Pitching screens are shaped like an L and protect the pitcher while allowing him the lane in which to throw. Protective screens are placed in front of first base during batting practice so the first basemen can field throws without being hit by a batted ball. Both of these provide protection from batted balls and make practice safer and more efficient.

The Tools of Ignorance

Anyone who has ever had the unique opportunity to crouch behind home plate for nine innings trying to catch or block everything that is thrown is struck at some point with two realizations. The first one is, "Boy am I glad I'm wearing all of this gear." And the second develops into something like this: "There must be an easier way to play this game!"

Catchers are the kids on your team who love to get dirty and want to be a constant part of the action. The equipment today is very well made and does a great job of protecting young catchers. So before these prospects know any better, take advantage of their ignorance and dress them in "the tools." The position is made for them. Look for youngsters who are physically tough and are natural leaders.

Uniforms

In most cases, your recreation department will provide a uniform for each player. Uniforms include a T-shirt top, midcalf-length pants with elastic cuffs, stirrups (special pullover socks), and a cap. However, if they are not provided, you or a designated parent can arrange a sign-up night at a local sports store where kids can be outfitted with a T-shirt (you can easily include a logo on the T-shirt), pants, and a hat. Sports stores will normally give significant discounts to teams for such an arrangement.

It's essential that orders are placed before the start of the season, so don't be reluctant to solicit the help of parents. They often are excited to pitch in and help where needed.

Questions and Answers

Q. I have 18 kids on my team. How do I deal with this large number?

A. Baseball is a team game that is learned primarily on an individual basis. The stress in practice is placed on honing the fundamental skills: fielding a ground ball, learning various throwing skills, swinging the bat. As a result, the majority of practice time is not spent performing "team drills"—drills that have 9 players active while 9 others stand and watch. Most of the defensive drills are set up for players to work in groups or pairs. So a team with 18 or more players can still work toward achieving your goal: every player having fun while learning and working hard at the skills and game of baseball.

However, when you do perform team drills and drills in which

Keeping Your Eye on the Ball (and Bats, and Everything Else): Delegate!

Carrying all of the equipment back and forth between the car and the field may seem like a daunting task for one person to handle. Here's the perfect opportunity for you to delegate responsibility. Assign players by position the job of carrying each equipment bag from your car to the field and back again after practice. The items to carry include the bat bag, ball bags, helmet bag, catcher's gear, and first-aid kit. Each week, change the rotation of jobs and instill in your players a sense of pride for doing their respective jobs well.

players are set at their positions, distribute the kids evenly among the positions. By practicing this way, you and the kids will become accustomed to sharing positions with teammates and, in addition, to sharing playing time come game day. Distribution of your players to the various positions also means increasing the size of your pitching staff. Adding even one more player to your team who can throw consistent strikes will unquestionably work to your advantage at some point during the season—whether throwing in a game or at batting practice.

Finally, with a large team you need to focus on running a disciplined and efficient batting practice. The batting practice format established in chapter 5 (see pages 74–75) is directed at a team of 15 players and includes players in various hitting stations, batting against live pitching, catching, and shagging batted balls. If you have more than 15 players, add to the number who are shagging balls and add an extra pitcher and catcher, if possible. Most importantly, if you have a large team, stick to the batting practice schedule, limit the number of pitches that each batter receives, and keep your players active.

Q. No one has volunteered to be the team manager, and I am feeling completely overwhelmed. What do I do?

A. Delegating a parent to be team manager would certainly free you from having to deal with a lot of details, but if no one is willing to help, you can manage this on your own. The key will be organization. First you will need to establish the phone tree, which will free you from ever having to call more than one or two players. And you need to do the schedule for where and when to meet for practices and games. You need to take care of these two items early. Also, don't feel shy about calling parents and asking them to get involved in the administrative details. Just because no one has volunteered for the whole job doesn't mean that parents would be unwilling to help with one or more specific projects if you ask them. Take charge and stress to them that the more they help, the better their child's experience will be.

Q. One of my players cannot afford to buy a glove. How should I deal with this?

A. It is very important that each player has a glove that he or she can use throughout the season. If a family cannot afford to buy a glove, talk to the parents about the situation and let them know that you do not want this impediment to prevent their son or daughter from having a great time as a member of the team, but make it clear that the youngster will need a glove. First, ask the parents if they know anybody who might be willing to lend a glove to them for the season. Let the parents know the approximate size to look for, and encourage them to settle for a glove that is disproportionately small or large only as the last resort. If this suggestion doesn't work, ask the parents if they would allow you to ask your other players whether any one of them might have an extra glove. If they give you permission, let your players know that they have the opportunity to help a teammate and strengthen the team. Often someone on the team has an extra glove at home that the player can use.

Q. Where do I find out the details of practice and game scheduling? Do I have to call coaches to set up games? Is this something I have to take care of myself, or does the league do it, or what?

A. It depends on whether your town or school sponsors the league. If the school sets it up, contact the athletic director or physical education teacher. If the town sponsors the league, talk to the director of the recreation department. You might find that everything is done for you, from field time to game scheduling. It is useful to have the names and phone numbers of the other coaches in case, for example, there is ever a question of game cancellation.

There are rules and details specific to each league that every new coach needs to learn about, so if your recreation department or school holds a league meeting, make every effort to attend. Not only is the information discussed in these meetings helpful, but the interaction with veteran coaches who attend such meetings is invaluable.

Q. I'm having trouble drafting my letter to parents about what I expect from the season. I don't want to offend anyone or hurt anyone's feelings.

A. Remember two things: one, this doesn't have to be the Gettysburg Address, and two, you are the leader of the team and the one responsible for setting its tone, goals, and rules. In a short letter, let the parents know how excited you are to be coaching, articulate your main goals of fun and development, and continually stress the positive. Though you may not be overly confident in your knowledge of the game, you are still the leader and the one from whom kids will learn not only baseball skills but also discipline and good training habits. Have someone else proofread your letter, and certainly feel free to use our sample letter on page 26.

Q. The league is providing little or no equipment. What should I do?

A. First, inform parents of the situation. Invite them to have their kids bring their own bats. Second, contact a local sports store that might be able to offer a deal on the equipment for local teams and/or because you are purchasing "in bulk." Third, solicit parental help in fund-raising. Contact local businesses and institutions, let them know your situation, and ask for donations or create a poster on which they can purchase advertising space.

CHAPTER 4

Essential Skills— and How to Teach Them

I have always loved baseball because it rewards those players who are taught correctly and who work hard at the fundamentals of the game. No other major sport has so many professional players who at first glance don't look like they belong. The reason is that proper fundamentals and lots of repetition can overcome being "too small" or "too slow." Anyone who has seen Nomar Garciaparra make an outstanding diving stop, or watched Ken Griffey Jr. make a catch against the wall, or marveled at the sight of a Mark McGwire home run must know that these spectacular plays represent countless numbers of hours spent learning the fundamentals of the game. Your players need to know that even your simplest drills are practiced by the major league players every day. Such drills introduce you and your players to the *fundamentals* of skill development.

Catching

The first thing that I teach any player, when it comes to fundamentals of the game, is how to catch a thrown or batted ball. Once a ball is batted, nothing can happen defensively until the ball is fielded. And once a throw has been made, no matter how accurate, it cannot be a successful play without the ball being caught. But despite the importance of catching, it is a skill that is often taken for granted at higher levels. A coach at the youth level, however, cannot make this mistake.

The Principles

The keys to catching include setting up the catch by moving to the ball, using two hands, and proper glove positioning.

Setting up the catch

As the ball is in the air, the fielder must try to position herself so that the ball is caught toward the middle of the body and at chest height, rather than just moving the glove side to side or up and down. This means that players need to be able to move laterally and get into a good athletic stance to catch the ball.

Using two hands

Catching the ball should be done, whenever possible, using both hands. A right-handed thrower catches with his left hand but secures the catch with

Left: When catching a thrown ball above the waist, step to the ball with the glove up and always, always catch with two hands.

Right: Keep the glove facing down when the throw is below the waist.

Left: After the catch, get your feet, hips, and shoulders perpendicular to the target and get the arm up in a cocked position.

Right: For a high throw, make sure the arm is fully extended and jump to the backhand side. This is one time that you want to catch one-handed.

A Ballplayer's Baby

There is no more valuable possession to a baseball player than his or her glove. Players often keep gloves for decades and treat their "leather" as if it were a baby. The most important characteristic of a glove, particularly at a young age, is its size. Your players need to find gloves that are big enough to properly catch the ball, but small and light enough for the players to handle.

Tell your players to get new or used fielders' gloves (rather than first-base gloves or catchers' gloves), regardless of the position they will play. That way they can learn to play various positions.

There are many theories for how to break in a glove, but I have always done it one way. First I rub glove oil into the leather. Then I place two baseballs on the spot where the index finger of the glove meets the pocket, close the fingers around the ball, and wrap the thumb over the fingers. I then use rubber bands or string to tie the glove shut in this position. After two days, I unwrap it and throw the ball over and over into the glove, trying to hit every time the specific spot where the ball had been while it was wrapped up. I then rewrap it and repeat this procedure every day for about a week. After this period, I begin using the glove to play catch, and slowly, over time, it loosens up. Oiling it once a month is always a good idea. It is also important to always keep a baseball in the glove when it is not in use. Otherwise the pocket flattens out and loses the rounded shape that is so inviting to a baseball.

the right hand by covering the pocket and limiting the chance of the ball popping out of the glove. A left-handed thrower catches with her right hand and secures with her left.

Glove work

Catching the ball in a perfect athletic stance and with two hands, however, is not always possible. A baseball player must be able to adjust to the ball with the positioning of the glove. A throw directed above the waist is caught with the fingers pointing up. A low throw directed below the waist is caught with the fingers pointing down and the heel facing up. A throw that comes directly at the waist, the most difficult type of stationary catch, forces a player to bend the knees and catch the ball at chest level with fingers pointing up. Finally, a ball above the player's head forces him to jump and make a one-handed catch. Catch this ball to the backhand. This particular catch requires full arm extension. Quick decision making and footwork are key to the proper positioning of the glove in these situations.

Footwork

After the catch is made, the player needs to organize her feet in preparation to throw. An outfielder uses a *crow-hop*, and an infielder uses a quicker *toe-to-heel hop*. Both of these techniques are described in the next section on throwing (see page 40), but it is important to realize that catching and throwing are most often meshed into one continuous activity and are not skills that are exclusive of one another.

Balls cannot always be caught while the player is in a stationary position. Running catches—catches made to the far glove-hand side or far throwing-hand side of the body—require specific glove work. Neither of these particular types of catches can be made using two hands. A catch made to the far glove-hand side—called a *forehand* catch—is made with the fingers below and the thumb on top. When making a forehand catch, the player reaches to the ball with the glove-side leg. A *backhand* catch is made to the far throwing-hand side of the body with the fingers above and the thumb below. To make this play, a player crosses his glove-side leg over the other leg and reaches toward the ball. As noted in the introduction, drills are numbered consecutively by type: warm-up (W), defense fundamentals (D), batting practice (B), and ending activity (E).

Drills

- Above, below, and at Waist High **W11**
- Wave Drill without Ball **D15**
- Wave Drill with Ball **D16**
- Ball to Throwing-Side Drill **W13**
- Backhand Drill **W14**
- Five Every Five **W15**
- Focus Drill **W16**
- Quick Hand Drill **W17**

Throwing

If Yogi Berra had been a coach, he probably would have said something like this: "The first thing I teach my kids is how to catch, and at the same time I teach 'em how to throw." But whereas kids come to the game of baseball needing to learn how to catch, the majority of them come with some background in throwing, whether rocks, snowballs, or baseballs. This can be good and bad. Some experience allows you to start with some of the groundwork already done, but more often than not, the groundwork has been built on a foundation of bad habits that must be broken. That's why I begin with the basics. At the youth level, whether you are throwing from the infield, from the outfield, as a catcher, or even as the pitcher, the proper fundamentals are basically the same.

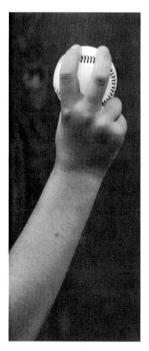

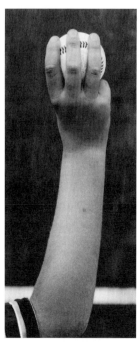

Left: The four-seam grip, back view. Two fingers run directly behind the ball with finger pads across the long seam. The ring finger stabilizes the ball.

Center: The four-seam grip, side view. Note that the thumb is under, and in front of the ball. Use a firm grip, but keep a loose wrist.

Right: Three-finger grip, back view. This grip works great for players whose hands are too small for a two-finger grip. Stabilize the ball with the little finger.

Overhand versus Sidearm: Which Is Better?

The most efficient and least stressful way to throw a baseball is with a three-quarter overhead motion. This gives the thrower a downward plane for power plus rotational forces (torque) of the trunk. Occasionally, a coach will find a player with a shoulder that has a restricted range of motion for the three-quarter angle of the arm. This player may have greater arm and hand speed (and less restriction) by throwing sidearm. If he develops proper sidearm throwing mechanics, he might be an effective relief pitcher or maybe a second baseman, but the sidearm motion is more fatiguing and stressful on the shoulder (posterior rotator cuff muscles) than the three-quarter overhand motion.

The Principles

Throwing is a fluid motion that involves very specific mechanics, but it can't be mechanical. The key components of a throwing motion include proper grip on the baseball, footwork, arm action, stride, release, and follow-through.

1. Grip

Most young players don't have hands big enough to hold the ball properly. That's okay. Players with relatively big hands can grab a baseball with two fingers (index and middle fingers) on top of the ball and the thumb underneath. But younger players with small hands can get away with placing three fingers on top of the ball (index, middle, and ring fingers) and a thumb on the side for support. A thrower should also try to "grab a seam." In other words, whether the player uses two fingers to throw or three, she feels with the pads of the fingers for a seam in order to provide a more reliable grip on the ball. The result of a proper grip is much greater throwing accuracy and more velocity.

2. Footwork

A right-handed thrower begins the motion by pointing his right foot, along with his shoulders and hips, perpendicular to the target. A lefty does the same thing, except she points her left foot, along with shoulders and hips, perpendicular to the target.

3. Arm Action

As the player prepares to throw, his hands begin together at chest height. As the stride leg begins moving toward the target, the hands break. The throwing hand makes an arc, moving from down to up until the elbow is shoulder height, the forearm is pointing upward, and the fingers are on top of the ball and pointing away from the target. This is called the *cocked position*—cocked and ready to throw. The other elbow also breaks to shoulder height. This process takes place while the stride foot (the left foot for right-handed throwers, and the right foot for lefties) reaches toward the target.

When I Say "Overhand," I Really Mean Three-Quarters

Many youth players are being taught to throw the ball with too much overhead angle. Experienced players actually throw in a three-quarter overhead angle, not directly overhead. Outfielders come the closest to overhand because they want the ball to carry and stay on a straight line by creating a 12 to 6 o'clock ball rotation. However, outfielders don't have to make very many long, hard throws every day.

The extreme overhand angle puts a lot of stress on the shoulder joint and often causes impingement of the biceps tendon or rotator cuff muscles. There is also much more stress on the lower spine because of the extreme tilt of the trunk as the thrower tries to get an overhand arm and body angle.

Stride, release, and follow-through

The stride foot lands and points toward the target. Once the stride foot hits, the hips and shoulders are rotated explosively to face the target, followed by the arm and ball. The fingers and ball are supposed to face away from the target in the cocked position, because after this body rotation, the fingers and ball are facing the target and ready to be released. When you see unusual rotation on the ball that resembles the look of a curveball, it probably means that the thrower's fingers are underneath the ball in the cocked position, and as a result, her fingers are on the side of the ball at the release point. The most effective and powerful release point is not actually "overhand" but is rather at a three-quarters delivery. After release, the arm continues down across the body and outside the stride leg, the rear foot rotates and ends up even with the stride foot, and the body is square to the target.

Transitions

In game situations, the transition from fielding to throwing must be quick yet smooth. Whether the situation involves an outfielder throwing after catching a fly ball, or an infielder firing to first base after fielding a ground ball, time is crucial. This transition process is known as "organizing the feet" in order to throw. Because outfielders often make long throws compared to infielders' shorter and quicker throws, each position has its own type of footwork.

Throwing Darts

One of the most obvious signs that one of your defensive players—whether a pitcher, an infielder, or even an outfielder—has lost his confidence throwing a ball accurately is by the fact that he looks like he is throwing darts. When a player becomes afraid of making an errant throw, he will often try to aim the ball to the target. This problem begins because the thrower does not properly extend the arm to the cocked position and does not aggressively rotate the body in order to throw the ball hard. Instead, he tries to guide the ball to the target and leaves behind the proper fundamentals of throwing. The result of aiming the ball is that, most often, throws lack velocity and end up well short of the target.

The solution is to tell that player to throw as hard as he can and to reassure him that it's okay if he makes a mistake going all out. In practice, give him a few extra chances to throw to first base or let him throw some pitches—nonthreatening situations—and let him "air out" his arm and experience the difference.

Drills:

- Five Every Five `W15`
- Focus Drill `W16`
- Quick Hand Drill `W17`
- Field and Throw `D6`
- Hot Potato `D8`
- Slow Rollers to Third Base `D9`
- Bobbled Ball Drill `D13`
- Dive Drill `D14`
- Wave Drill without Ball `D15`
- Wave Drill with Ball `D16`
- Outfielder's Ground Ball Techniques without Ball `D18`
- Outfielder's Ground Ball Techniques with Ball `D19`
- Relay Drill `D22`

Learning to Throw Effectively

Virtually all young children begin throwing balls by pushing the ball away from their bodies rather than using hip and body rotation to generate power, primarily because their abdominal and hip flexor muscles lack strength. As they get older and stronger, children become better throwers through trial and error and years of baseball practice—they achieve harder, faster, and farther throws through proper trunk rotation. Children who don't play baseball early or long enough to learn proper arm action or how to close up their bodies and use the power generated from good hip and torso rotation to power their throws often rely on pushing the ball from an open position that they used as a young child. But even children with relatively less muscle mass can learn to throw with sound mechanics if they are taught proper footwork, trunk rotation, and arm action at an early age. Their throwing muscles may not be as strong, and thus not as explosive as throwers with longer experience and more developed muscles, but they can learn proper throwing mechanics and become very accurate and efficient throwers.

Outfield crow-hop

The crow-hop allows an outfielder to gather momentum while properly positioning the feet to throw. A right-handed thrower, after making a catch, steps forward on to his left foot and hops forward, turning his body perpendicular to the target, crossing his right leg over and in front of the left. When the right foot lands, it should be perpendicular to the target. Once in this position, the mechanics are identical to the basic throwing motion just described—the hands break, the stride leg points to the target, the arm cocks, the hips and shoulders rotate, the ball is released, and the motion of the arm, leg, and body follows through. A left-handed thrower simply uses the opposite footwork.

Infield toe-to-heel hop

The technique of toe-to-heel hop allows infielders to quickly gain momentum toward first base or whatever target to which they might be throwing. After an infielder fields a ground ball, and as she comes up out of her stance, she pushes off her rear, throwing-side foot (right foot for right-handed throwers, left foot for lefties), shuffling it toward the front foot. The toe of the rear foot kicks the heel of the front foot, the rear foot plants perpendicular to the target, momentum has been built, and the feet are in line for a strong, accurate throw.

Infield Defense

The vast majority of errors made in baseball from the youth leagues on up to the majors occur in the infield. Fielding a ground ball is difficult because of the ground's irregularity. Bad bounces can easily result in errors, but the expectation of a bad hop can also cause an error when the ball *bounces true*. Anyone who remembers Bill Buckner's famous error in the 1986 World Series remembers the slow-rolling ground ball that trickled through his legs, allowing the winning run to score for the New York Mets. Even though the ball was rolling along the ground, he expected it to bounce up. As a result, his raised glove allowed room enough for that infamous grounder to slip through his legs. Boston will never be the same.

The majority of errors, however, are the result of improper technique. The solution is found in practicing correct fundamentals.

This infielder is set in a good athletic stance and is ready for anything.

The Principles

The fundamentals of fielding a ground ball include three components: preparation, good body positioning, and quick but soft hands.

Preparation (Stance and Approach)

As the pitch is being delivered, each fielder shifts his weight to the balls of his feet and starts moving slightly forward. This type of preparation enables the fielder to make quick and aggressive movement toward the ball when it is hit. The two objectives of this movement are to get to the ball as quickly as possible and, more importantly, to field the easiest bounce. The player's hands are together and in front of the body, his body is square to the plate, and his eyes are on the batter and her swing.

The Athletic Stance

Movement ought to be toward the ball, but as the ball gets near, the fielder needs to assume a good fielding position. This "athletic stance" is relatively the same positioning a defender would assume playing basketball and

What Is the Athletic Stance?

Each sport requires distinctive mechanics and unique skills, but I know of no active sport that is properly played in an upright position. Sports are to be played in the *athletic stance*—the optimal body position for quickness and balance. A player in the athletic position has her weight slightly forward on the balls of the feet. The feet are just wider than shoulder width apart, and the knees are flexed. The upper body is straight, eyes are up, and the arms and hands are relaxed and ready for action. Impress upon your players that they play in games the way they practice. As a result, encourage them to practice in the athletic stance and see them improve in the games.

Keep on Your Toes

Our coach in high school used to pummel us with ground balls until we learned to *attack the ball*—to always meet it after moving forward. We had a great defense, and I was lucky enough that season, even as a third baseman, to have avoided being seriously injured by a ground ball, a tribute to his coaching. One day, in a walk-through type practice the day before a big playoff game, I asked for a couple ground balls, just for extra work. The mellow mood of the practice must have affected my approach to fielding, and I found myself playing the baseball on my heels. The second ground ball took a funny hop, one that I surely would have smothered had I charged it aggressively, and it caught me underneath my chin. The ball knocked me backward, and the seams from the ball split open my chin. I never forgot the lesson I learned that day, whether as a player or a coach: play the ball aggressively, don't let the ball play you, or get hurt. It's as simple as that.

involves the following components: feet are wider than shoulder width apart; weight is still on the balls of the feet; knees are bent to 90 degrees; back remains straight; and body is square to the baseball. Finally, the player positions herself to receive the ball at the midline of her body with the hands out in front of the body.

A common error among infielders is to fall back on the heels. This disrupts balance and makes adjusting to irregular bounces very difficult, whereas remaining on the balls of the feet improves quickness. Another common problem is bending at the waist and not at the knees. The deep knee bend creates better balance and allows the fielder to stay down on the ball. The fielder should look the ball right into the glove.

Keep the approach to the ball controlled and balanced, and line up the ground ball.

3. Hands

Hand positioning is the final component and contributes greatly in handling bad hops. Fielding a ground ball must be performed with two hands whenever possible, and many drills that I use don't involve the use of a glove, making the habit of using two hands essential. When a player is in the proper stance with knees bent and weight forward, the hands can then extend outward and downward so that they make a 45-degree angle with the ground. Thus, the player is fielding the ball *not* directly between the legs but, rather, out in front of his body. This allows for him to track the ball visually into the glove. It also enables him to use *soft hands*. This means "giving" with the baseball, as if he were fielding an egg, and funneling it softly up and into the navel area. The result is like having the ground ball roll into a pillow rather than a brick wall.

Feet are wide, glove fingers on the ground with the glove out in front, and the bare hand ready to secure the ball.

Fielding the ball at the midline of the stance and with two hands is not always possible, however. Ground balls hit to the far right or left of the body require forehands and backhands—plays made with only the outstretched glove hand. A player needs to approach both these types of ground balls with her glove near to the ground, because adjusting upward is much easier and quicker than trying to adjust to a ball that skips under the glove. Just like catching a ball close to the forehand or backhand sides of the body, the leg on the glove-hand side of the body extends toward the ball. A *forehand* involves extending the fingers to the ground with the palm up, whereas a *backhand* extends in front of the body with the webbing and thumb down. Keeping the glove open to the ball is the challenge of a backhand, so offer special praise and encouragement when backhands are made successfully or even attempted. They are the most difficult of infield plays.

The major impediment to proper technique among young players is the fear of being hit by the ground ball. As a result of this fear, kids may play on their heels, jerk their heads away from the play as the ball arrives, or play the ball to the side of their bodies, often with a leg sticking out. All

Left: A forehand grab. The fielder stays low and keeps the glove out in front of his feet, glove fingers down.

Right: The backhand. The fielder stays low with the glove out. Note the foot and leg position.

Conquering Fear of the Ball: Fielders

All young players, and many older players, have a real fear of being hit by batted balls, particularly hard ground balls. The first thing players need to learn is how to catch a thrown ball properly—a ball that is thrown low, high, to the glove side, to the throwing-hand side, and directly at them. Using an Incredi-ball (sponge-filled ball) to practice drills will help players become comfortable with these skills.

Teaching your players good fielding position and how to approach a ground ball will also go a long way toward alleviating both the fear of being hit and their chances of being caught unprepared. Roll ground balls using the Incredi-ball until the players gain confidence in their fielding techniques. The more the fielders get their hands out in front and stay low, the better they can track the ball into the glove and protect themselves. Next roll regular baseballs to the players; then hit short (40-foot) easy *fungoes*, or soft, practice fly balls. Rolled ground balls and short fungoes should be a part of every practice.

three of these defensive tactics are less effective than the fundamental method. Playing the ball on one's heels, as opposed to being on the balls of the feet, takes the hands out of a good forward position and limits a fielder's ability to adjust to the bouncing ball. Jerking the head away is dangerous because the eyes can no longer follow the ball. That's a bad idea. And the one-legged stop technique most often results in a ground ball that caroms off the shin. The best *and safest* technique is also the most aggressive and fundamental. By initially charging the ball in preparation for the easy bounce, and by being in front of the baseball with weight on the balls of the feet, knees bent, and hands out in front of the body, a player greatly increases his quickness and reaction time. The lower the eyes and head, the better the chance of the glove protecting the face in case of a bad hop and for making a good play.

Tag outs and put outs

In addition to fielding the ball, infielders are also responsible for tagging runners who slide into the base. Players making a tag straddle the base and sweep the tag using a backhand technique. This protects the ball from being knocked out of the glove and allowing the runner to be called "safe." The glove should also be out in front of the base, and the fielder should bend her knees into an athletic stance for balance, agility, and so she can move away from the runner after the tag.

Finally, it is important to know and teach both an infielder's throw and the *punch throw*. An infielder's throw is more compact and quicker than that of an outfielder or a pitcher, but it incorporates similar mechanics. The punch throw is an underhand toss that is used at short range and most often between the shortstop and second baseman in making force-outs at second base and in turning double plays. When a player is within approximately 10 feet of his target, he can use this technique. A player making a punch takes a long step toward the target with the glove-side foot and holds the ball with the fingers underneath and next to the hip. He keeps the glove

Top left: Making the tag. The fielder straddles the base and protects the ball by sweeping with a backhand tag. Note that the glove is out in front of the base.

Top right: An infielder's throw. Keep the fingers behind the ball and the throwing motion compact.

Bottom left: For an underhand toss, step to the receiver and keep your wrist firm and fingers under the ball.

Bottom right: The double play toss. The shortstop steps to the second baseman and shows the ball before the throw. Note the second baseman's foot is on the base.

Drills:

- Ground Ball Work D1
- All at Shortstop D5
- Field and Throw D6
- Knockout D7
- Hot Potato D8
- Slow Rollers to Third Base D9
- Middle-Infield Double Play D10
- Turning Double Plays D11
- Ground Balls at Positions D12
- Bobbled Ball Drill D13
- Dive Drill D14

in close to the chest to clearly show the recipient the ball. He then tosses the ball to the fielder without breaking his wrist so that the action is like making an uppercut punch. He then follows the punch by following through and stepping toward the target with the throwing-side foot.

Outfield Defense

Baseball is a game of wonderful images, one of which is the sight of a towering fly ball that comes to rest lazily in the waiting glove of an outfielder. This skill, however, is often difficult for the young player, who may lose her balance and bearings while having to look upward. There is, then, no substitute for hitting or even throwing a lot of fly balls in practice and teaching the fundamentals of outfield play.

The Principles

The three keys for playing fundamental outfield defense involve the first step, footwork, and using two hands.

First step

The first step in reacting to a fly ball is half the battle when it comes to making a good play. Experienced outfielders develop the ability to break immediately, at the crack of the bat, in the direction of the ball. But for a young player, it requires at least *one step of time* to determine whether the ball is going to land in front of him or behind. In other words, the time it takes to judge a fly ball's direction is about the time it takes to make a step In what direction, then, should the player step? The first step in fielding a fly ball ought to be backward because it is easier to react to a ball in front of you than a ball that is going over your head. Quite simply, you can run forward faster than you can backward, so it makes sense that your outfielders' first step should be in the direction that is most difficult to run.

Left: Catch the ball above the head, and use two hands. The fielder's feet are set and his body is behind the ball.

Center: The outfield crow-hop. The back foot crosses in front of and beyond the stride foot. The rear foot is perpendicular to the target.

Right: The follow-through. Stride directly toward the target, body weight into the throw.

Furthermore, a ball that falls in front of a player is much less dangerous than one that lands over his head and rolls away from the fielder. The former results in a single while the latter will mean extra bases.

Footwork

By proper footwork I mean two things: taking a direct angle to the ball and sprinting to the place where it will land. Youth-level math and science classes teach that the shortest distance between two points is a straight line—so too must youth-level baseball. The Wave Drill (see drills D15 and D16 on pages 131–34) described in chapter 10 teaches the footwork involved in taking the most direct angle to the place where the baseball will land. Once the outfielder has correctly judged the fly ball and is running the most direct route, she runs to the place where it will land as quickly as possible. You will sometimes see major league outfielders drift under lazy fly balls and catch the ball on the run, but this is not the example you want your players to follow. When someone is running, his head will move up and down, and it becomes difficult to focus steadily on the descending ball. Instead, your players should sprint to the spot where the ball will land, set their feet, and make the catch. This will eliminate the bobbing head problem and will allow them more time to make any last-second adjustments to the fly ball. These adjustments are often necessary, particularly if there is wind to affect the ball.

Using two hands

Finally, a fly ball must be caught, if at all possible, above the head and with two hands. Once again, players in the major leagues do not provide the example your players should follow. Teach them to extend, but bend, their arms so that they make the catch just above their foreheads, but not blocking the line to the ball. It's also essential that they wrap their throwing hands around the glove pocket as it closes on the ball. In executing these proper fundamentals, your players can take pride in the fact that they do it better than the pros.

Of course, it's impossible to settle under every fly ball and to make every catch with two hands. Some require running one-hand catches or even diving plays, but these are plays that cannot be executed with any kind of consistency until the fundamentals are ingrained. The drills previously mentioned—Above, below, and at the Waist (see drill W11 on pages 122–23) and the Wave Drills (see drills D15 and D16 on pages 131–34)—work on forehands, backhands, and running catches. As some of your outfielders become better with stationary and thrown fly balls, force them into running-catch situations. Many of the drills will work on this skill, but in general it's important that your outfielders run straight lines toward the ball and watch the ball land in their gloves as they are running. However, I've always said that I would rather my team make all the routine plays and none of the spectacular ones than make a few of both.

Right: The reliable block technique. Drop to the glove-side knee and keep the glove in front.

Below: An infield stance works as well. Keep the feet wide and the body square to the ball, hands out in front.

Finally, it's essential that your outfielders communicate when the ball is in the air. To avoid collisions, particularly on balls that are hit between two fielders, the fielders need to "call the ball." By this I mean that whoever is confident that she can catch it yells, "I've got it!" In order to complete the line of communication, the other fielder should follow with, "You take it!" As a general rule, the center fielder has the last word in the outfield, which means that if she calls for the ball, the other fielders should back up the play. On the other hand, a fielder who does call for the ball must feel that she has a very good chance of making the catch. In order to avoid making the early and wrong call, players should not call for the ball until it has started downward.

In addition to other fielders, players need to know the location of objects such as fences or other possible hazards. Teammates of a player in pursuit of a fly ball should tell him how much space he has to make the catch. It is the responsibility of the player in pursuit to first find the ball, next find the fence, and then pick up the ball again. Ideally he can put a hand on the fence and then move away from it, but often there's not time. As the coach, you have the primary responsibility of teaching communication and caution. This is certainly a situation in which it's better to be safe than sorry.

Fielding outfield ground balls incorporates the same fundamental principles as in the infield, except that outfielders often have less pressure to make a quick play. Unless the outfielder is trying to throw someone out at a base, the player's job is simply to keep the ball in front of her and to prevent the runner from advancing. Thus, you should emphasize staying low and squaring up to the ball, while the more skilled outfielders on your team can work on charging the ball with the intent of throwing a runner out at a base. The three types of techniques for fielding ground balls in the outfield that young players should learn are the block technique, infielder's position, and the do-or-die charge.

Block technique

The block technique is normally used when the batter hits a single with no one else on base. The outfielder simply wants to keep the ball in front of him, throw the ball back into the infield, and effectively prevent the runner from advancing to second base. A player using the block technique charges toward the ball; he has plenty of time, so he drops to the knee on his throwing-hand side and squares his body to the ball. He keeps his glove out in front of his body, but as long as the ball stays in front of him, fielding it cleanly is not a priority.

Infielder's technique

With runners on base, an outfielder should again make sure to keep the ball in front of her, but with a greater sense of urgency. She should charge the ground ball and set up in an infielder's athletic stance. This means knees bent, back straight, hands out in front of the body and on the ground, and weight on the balls of the feet. This puts the outfielder in a better position to throw, should a runner try to advance an extra base.

Do-or-die charge

With a base runner on second base, and one that represents a key run in the game, an outfielder needs to risk everything to throw the runner out at home. The outfielder aggressively charges the base hit and attempts to field the ground ball on the glove-hand side of the body. He uses the glove alone and fields the ball out in front of the foot on the glove-hand side. The fielder stays low, flexes his knees, and bends at the waist. He then goes immediately into a crow-hop and throws to the relay person who is lined up with home plate. This play is extremely risky since the ball can easily skip past the sprinting outfielder, allowing any other runners to advance at least one extra base. For this reason, this technique should only be used by more advanced players and in "do-or-die" situations late in the game.

Drills:
- Wave Drill without Ball `D15`
- Wave Drill with Ball `D16`
- Quarterback Drill `D17`
- Outfielder's Ground Ball Techniques (without Ball) `D18`
- Outfielder's Ground Ball Techniques with Ball `D19`
- Batted Fly Balls `D20`
- Communication Drill `D21`

The do-or-die charge. Charge the ball hard but get it under control. Stay low and keep your knees flexed.

Finally, outfielders should try to keep throws as low and as straight on a line as possible and to avoid throws that are high and loopy. Young players may think that a throw reaching its destination on the fly is better than one that bounces, but this is not the case. A low, hard throw that reaches a base or relay person on one or two bounces takes much less time than a lofted throw that travels higher in the air. As your outfielders develop, encourage them to use the crow-hop (described on page 46) and throw on a line to the cut-off man.

Team Defense

In addition to individual defense, there are fundamental concepts that are important to know in playing good team defense. Though at higher levels team defense may include proper execution of special plays, the fundamentals are the same at all levels and center on making good decisions. You need to train your players to make good decisions such as throwing to the correct base, backing up other fielders, etc., a process that begins with a *conservative* approach to defense.

The Principles

There are many strategies and plays to defend against as a team, but the fundamental concepts of team defense include getting the easiest out on each play, avoiding unnecessary throws, and having a field general who guides the fielding.

Get the easiest out

Outs are a precious commodity at the youth level, and they should be made whenever possible. When the lead runner represents the go-ahead run in the last inning, your defense may need to take risks in order to cut her down. But under normal circumstances, getting a sure out is the wisest strategy. Imagine the following scenario: Your team is on defense, it is the second inning, and there is no score. There is a runner on third base with no outs, and the batter hits a ground ball to your shortstop, who fields the ball cleanly. The runner on third breaks for home . . . what should your shortstop do? The game is early, one run means very little in a youth league game, where scores are often quite high. Plus, the chances of your shortstop making a perfect throw to home and your catcher catching the ball and making the tag on the sprinting runner before he reaches the plate are pretty slim. Instead, your shortstop should make the relatively simple throw to first base and get a sure out.

Avoid unnecessary throws

A successful throw requires two things done well: an accurate throw and a completed catch. Thus, every time a throw is made, the potential for an error is high. Furthermore, the consequence of an errant throw or missed catch often means that all base runners will advance an extra base. Consequently, the proper and conservative approach is to encourage your players to avoid unnecessary throws—throws that have a very small chance of getting an out. The most common example of this type of situation occurs when a ground ball is misplayed, bobbled, and finally picked up by an infielder. The problem is that during the time it took to pick up the ball, the runner advanced well down the first-base line and is nearing the base. The infielder is now faced with a split-second decision: should she throw or not? If she chooses to throw in this situation, the throw is often wild and gets by the first baseman, allowing the runner to advance to second base. This situation is not cut-and-dried, however. Often there is still time to pick up the bobbled ball and throw the runner out, but the added pressure wreaks havoc on a young and tense ballplayer. The Bobbled Ball Drill (see drill D13 on page 131) works on developing poise and good judgment in this precise situation.

The field general

As a coach, you want one player in the outfield and one player in the infield who will take responsibility for keeping the defense alert and aware of what to do should the ball come to them. This "field general" is often the shortstop in the infield and the center fielder in the outfield, and with each new batter that comes up he calls out the situation. For example, with a runner on first base and one out, the shortstop would call to his fellow infielders: "One out! The play is to second base, but make sure you get an out!" On the same play, the center fielder would yell: "One out! On a

Fly-Ball Priority System

This system is designed so that fielders will have no doubt who has the right of way to catch a fly ball. Generally there is no doubt, but this system comes into play when more than one player is able to catch the ball, or when more than one fielder has called for the ball.

Position	Primary Fielder (priority over other positions)	Secondary Fielder (concedes to other positions)
1. pitcher	no one	all infielders, catcher
2. catcher	pitcher	1B, 3B
3. 1B	catcher, pitcher	2B, 3B, RF
4. 2B	1B, P	SS, any outfielder
5. 3B	C, P, 1B	SS, LF
6. SS	all infielders, P	all outfielders
7. LF	all infielders	CF
8. CF	all infielders and outfielders	no one
9. RF	all infielders	CF

The shortstop is "primary" over all infield positions; the center fielder is "primary" over everyone and "secondary" to no one.

Drills:
- Relay Drill D22
- Bunt Rotation D23
- Covering on a Steal D24
- Infield Practice D25
- Situations Off Fungo Hits E1

ground ball, the play is to third base! On a fly ball, the play is to second!" You will find that certain players enjoy such a role, whereas others would feel pressured in it. During practice sessions find the players that can fill this role as field general, you can create a rotating schedule between them of who is in charge for what inning. Situations Off Fungo Hits (drill E1), Soft-Toss Scrimmage (drill E2), and Full Scrimmage (drill E3), drills described on pages 146–47 of chapter 12, are good opportunities to have field generals practice their role as leaders. It is crucial, however, that you stress to them that their job is to call out the situation and to encourage their teammates, never to criticize or become arrogant. Continually monitor how they perform in this role throughout the entire season.

Playing good team defense also includes proper bunt coverage, defending against stealing, and setting up a simple relay system from the outfield to the infield. Drills that work on these various plays are described in detail in chapter 10 (see Relay Drill, D22; Bunt Rotation Drill, D23; Covering on a Steal, drill D24; and Infield Practice, drill D25 on pages 136–40) in the section called Team Defense. Field generals can also work on calling out the situations in these specific drills.

Pitching

Pitching, like batting, is much easier for older kids with greater strength and physical development than it is for players at the youth level. But this does not mean that younger players should not learn proper throwing mechanics. It does mean, however, that coaches should control the amount that pitchers throw. Players between the ages of 6 and 9 should be restricted to 45 to 55 pitches in a game per week, and those between 10 and 12 should be held to 70 game pitches per week. These numbers do not include pitches thrown in practice and in warm-up.

The Principles

The primary goal for every pitcher is control—throwing strikes. But too often at ballparks one can hear coaches yelling, "Just throw strikes!" That is normally "just" what pitchers are trying to do, but they struggle because they do not know the proper fundamentals of pitching. The essential components of the pitching motion include the stance and

The foot pivot. Spike pivot in front of and parallel to the rubber.

windup, balance point, arm action, stride, trunk rotation, release, and follow-through.

Stance and windup

A right-handed pitcher usually begins on the right half of the rubber, and a left-handed pitcher from the left side. This position helps the pitcher stride in a straight line toward home plate. She ignites the motion with a *short*, rocker step backward with the stride foot (left foot for right-handed pitchers and right foot for lefties) at a 45-degree angle and positions her pivot foot in front of the rubber.

The proper pitcher's stance: toes in front of the rubber, body relaxed and square to home plate.

Balance point

The pitcher then lifts the stride leg (no higher than the belt) and closes the front hip so that the shoulders and hips are perpendicular to home plate and the knee points toward third base for right-handed pitchers and toward first base for left-handers. The posting leg should be fairly straight, and the pitcher should be balanced. The Fives Drill (drill B8 on page 144 of chapter 11) works on holding this balance point for 3 seconds before continuing to the plate. Being too far forward or too far back, and hence out of balance, is going to create problems in the throwing motion. Make sure that all of your pitchers come to this balance point before allowing the body to rush forward.

Arm action

As the stride leg starts downward, the hands break from the midline of the body. The throwing hand goes down, back, and up toward the cocked position in one continuous motion, keeping the fingers on top of the ball. The glove hand moves forward and upward toward the hitter. Again, in the Fives Drill (drill B8) pitchers work on throwing just from the cocked position. This position is reached after the stride foot has landed and both arms are up and ready to throw.

Stride

The stride leg should go "down-and-out" toward the plate, not "out-and-down." In the first instance, the leg moves directly toward the plate and allows the hips to stay closed longer, generating more power and creating less stress on the arm. The second technique causes the body to "fly open"

Left: The balance point, front view. The posting leg is straight and firm, the flexed knee high, hips and shoulders perpendicular to the plate with the knee pointing to third base, the shoulders level, and the eyes on the catcher's mitt.

Right: The balance point, side view. The head is over posting leg for good balance and the hands are together.

and puts undue stress on the pitcher's shoulder. The stride leg should be stable and the knee bent when it lands, and the stride foot should point toward home plate. Stride length measured from the rubber to the toe of the stride foot should be close (about 90 percent) to the pitcher's height.

Rotation and release

As the stride foot lands, the lead elbow (glove hand) pulls down and outside the lead hip. The hips and shoulders rotate explosively, the throwing elbow is at shoulder height, the arm whips around toward the plate, and the ball is released.

Follow-through

After the release, the throwing arm continues toward the plate and then moves down and outside the stride leg. Weight is on the stride leg. Both feet should end up in an even and squared position to the plate in a good fielding position. After the ball is released, the pitcher simply becomes another infielder and thus should be balanced and ready.

Forget the curve

Coaches and young pitchers often ask whether throwing curveballs is a good idea for players at the youth level. The answer is simple: No! First of all, throwing curveballs, even when done properly, adds strain to the elbow and adjoining tendons and ligaments. Exposing young players to this risk is

Top left: Cocked and ready. The throwing elbow is at shoulder height, fingers are on top of the ball with the palm facing shortstop, and the front elbow is aligned with home plate.

Top right: Stride directly toward home plate with the striding knee flexed. Shoulders remain aligned to the plate.

Bottom left: Rotate hips and shoulders so they're square to the plate.

Bottom right: In the follow-through the head and shoulders are outside the stride leg. The weight is on the stride leg as the rear leg comes through for balance.

simply not worth it. Secondly, kids can become consumed with "throwing junk" and, as a result, sacrifice learning the proper mechanics of throwing that will both preserve their arms for the long haul and will make them better pitchers in the future. There is still no pitch as effective or as intimidat-

Drills:
- Fives Drill B8
- Live Hitting B6

ing as a good, hard fastball—and that is what your players should be trying to master. Instead of tampering with curveballs, have your pitchers work on spotting their fastballs on the inside and outside corners of the plate and on altering the speed of their fastballs in order to disrupt the timing of opposing batters. Cy Young once said that "hitting is timing, and pitching is simply disrupting that timing." One does not need a curveball to do that.

Pitching is an art that is full of mechanical steps, but it must be performed fluently and without hesitation. Emphasize the different steps of the motion in practice and in the Fives Drill (drill B8 on page 144), but allow your pitchers to just throw in the games. Advice on their mechanics should be given in small doses and only to those pitchers that you think can understand what it is you're talking about. Otherwise, encourage them to throw and have fun with a focused and intense attitude.

Playing Catcher

Catcher is a crucial and a difficult position. Encourage any players on your team who show an interest in catching and continually reinforce their efforts, because finding a catcher is sometimes not easy. They will quickly find that it is hard, tiring play, but very rewarding.

The Principles

The greatest deterrent for young players from playing catcher is the fear of the ball. On the other hand, one of the great lures is the chance to wear all

Left: Ready to receive: wide stance, setting a good target, and the throwing hand protected behind the mitt.

Right: Don't try to catch a ball in the dirt—just make sure you block it.

that equipment. "The tools of ignorance" (see sidebar, page 31) are designed to keep the catcher very safe if he sticks to the fundamentals of catching.

Remain square to the pitch

This is the catcher's first rule. All the equipment—chest protector, neck guard, face mask, and helmet, and a cup for boys—is designed to protect the player's front. As the pitch is delivered, the catcher comes up into a crouch with feet wider apart and slightly staggered.

Protect your hand

The catcher should also develop the habit of keeping her throwing hand clenched in a relaxed fist and behind the mitt. The mitt provides a clear target. If the pitch is thrown in the dirt, the catcher needs to drop to her knees, straighten her back, and block the hole between her legs with the mitt. This also brings the chin, mask, and eyes down and directly over the pitch. It's crucial, at this point, that the catcher does not turn her body and stab with the mitt. This exposes her unprotected side and increases the risk of injury. The image a catcher should have of herself is not that of an infielder who tries to catch the ball cleanly in the glove, but rather as a wall that keeps the ball from going to the backstop.

Set up properly

The catcher should set up approximately 3 feet behind the center of the plate. He should make an open target with the mitt at the approximate height of the batter's kneecaps. It is crucial, for the safety of the catcher, that he not lunge for the pitch or slide too far forward when blocking a ball in the dirt. Either of these miscues can result in getting struck by a swing that is not only dangerous to the catcher but also results in the batter being awarded first base (the infraction is called "catcher's interference").

Catcher is a fun and ideal position for the tough players who are leaders and who love to get dirty and work up a sweat. The equipment made today and the slower speed at which the youth game is played make catching quite safe. Because very few of your players will have had any experience catching, you can feel free, then, to recruit players to put on the tools of ignorance and give it a shot.

Batting

Though some players will play infield and some outfield, others will catch, and a few will pitch—*all* of your players will have to bat. And the majority of them will love it. It is, however, a very difficult skill, and it requires a great deal of work and practice time to develop in your players. Batting may be difficult for kids because of a lack of physical development, being afraid

Drills:
- Block the Ball **B9**
- Fives Drill **B8**
- Infield Practice **D25**
- Live Hitting **B6**

Conquering Fear of the Ball: Catchers

Catchers need to be taught specific receiving techniques and drills, first in an upright (standing) position and then from a crouch.

Step 1: Use Incredi-balls and have your catcher dress in full gear. Teach him proper glove action and footwork for pitches to various locations, including in the dirt and blocking techniques. Remind him also to protect his throwing hand.

Step 2: Once he's comfortable behind the plate, put a batter in the batter's box but tell her not to swing; instead, the batter should let the pitches go by so that the catcher learns how to focus on the pitch and not be distracted by the batter's presence.

Step 3: Have the batter swing through the pitches but intentionally miss so that the catcher learns to visually track the pitch to the mitt without flinching, turning his head, or blinking his eyes. First use an Incredi-ball and then switch to a regular baseball.

Step 4: Have the catcher catch live batting practice.

of the ball, and improper technique. Some batters may rarely make contact in a game, but they can always experience progress and success through the basic, and helpful, drills designed for practice. Remain positive with each player, record everyone's development in the growth book, and encourage everyone toward improvement and a sense of accomplishment.

No two swings are alike, and no one person has the perfect swing. Ken Griffey Jr. and Tony Gwynn are both great hitters, but they couldn't have more different swings. Nevertheless, there are bad habits and good habits, and the good ones come from learning the proper fundamentals of batting.

The Principles

Batting includes six main components: the mental approach, grip, stance, launch position, swing, and follow-through.

A good grip on the bat calls for aligning the middle knuckles of both hands. Grasp the bat more firmly with the bottom hand.

The mental approach

You can recognize those players who were born to hit. They are the players who love to swing a bat and who even love walking around with a bat in hand. They tend to have an aggressive, confident, and positive approach to the game. But hitting isn't only innate. As the coach, you can instill this aggressive approach to batting in your players. When a batter walks up to the plate—unless you instruct her to be especially selective or to "take" a pitch—she should be thinking one thing: "HIT!" She can't be thinking about mechanics and batting techniques, and she can't even worry about striking out. Concentration on these details is done in practice. The game is the time to think positive—about hitting the ball hard. The mental characteristics of a good hitter are

- Aggressiveness: "think hit"
- Determination: "concentrate on the job at hand"
- Courage: "I have no fear of the ball, and no fear of failure"
- Self-discipline: "only swing at strikes"
- Concentration: " my bat on the ball"
- Ability to relax: "this is fun; this is my time to shine."
- Confidence: "I can do it!"

Grip

The bat should be held in the fingers, not in the palm. An indicator of the proper grip is having the second knuckles of both hands line up while holding the bat. The bat should be held firmer and deeper in the bottom hand. This may feel awkward at first for kids who are used to gripping the bat back in their palms like a club, but it frees up the wrists tremendously and is crucial in developing a level swing and for increasing swing speed, which results in more power.

Stance

Stances vary widely throughout the game of baseball, but it's crucial that each batter feel in balance and comfortable in her stance as she waits for the ball to be released. Feet should be slightly wider than shoulder width apart and roughly perpendicular to the pitcher. Though foot positioning varies, a young player should keep her front foot even with, slightly in front of, or slightly behind the front edge of the plate. Knees are bent, and the body and arms must remain level, loose, and relaxed. Hands stay back in front of the rear shoulder, and both eyes are level and focused on the pitcher.

A proper stance calls for aligning the feet and body with the pitcher, keeping the eyes, shoulders, and knees level, and both eyes focused on the pitcher.

Matching Bat and Batter

Every player who comes up to bat dreams of hitting it out of the park, but budding Sammy Sosas should start small and smart—a young hitter should use a bat that he can handle, which means a short, light bat that is well balanced. Swing speed, not bat weight, is the key to hitting the ball hard. Most young players are not physically strong enough to develop and generate a lot of rotational force, so until they reach approximately 13 to 14 years old, many players don't swing very efficiently. That's why a light, well-balanced bat is the key to a good, solid swing for young players.

Get a Grip! How to Hold the Bat

Most hitters should choke up on the bat an inch or so for better balance. The more the bat is balanced, the better the bat control and the greater the swing speed. Here's how: With the bottom hand (lead arm), grip the bat like you would grip an axe. Then take the top hand and line your middle knuckles up between the second and third knuckles of the bottom hand. Do not grip the top hand on the bat as deeply or as firmly as the bottom hand. The hands and forearm muscles should be relatively relaxed until the batter starts the swing forward.

Launch position

Though stances vary, all hitters should come to a fairly similar launch position—a position that is fueled and ready to launch into the swing as the pitcher winds and throws. As the stride foot lands and is closed to the pitch, the hands move backward so that there is tension felt in the lead arm (the left arm of a right-handed batter and the right arm of a left-handed batter). This tension is as if a rubber band, looped around the toe of the stride foot and attached to the bottom hand, were stretched in order to create power. The bat is tilted so that the top hand is closer to the pitcher than the bottom hand, but the bat should not be wrapped behind the batter's neck. The stride should be 2 to 5 inches long and toward the pitcher. With the hands back at armpit height, the batter's weight should be primarily on the back leg, with the stride foot acting as if it were testing ice on a pond. Thus far, neither the hips nor the shoulders should have opened to the ball but instead remain closed. This loads up the power that will be transferred into the swing as the body weight is transferred forward with the start of the swing.

Left: The launch. The batter's stride foot is down, weight is on the rear leg, and hands are armpit high. Note that the top hand is closer to the pitcher than the bottom hand.

Right: The swing: eyes on the contact point, weight evenly distributed, rear knee rotating.

Uppercut: The Young Batter's Nemesis

The most common batting problem among young players is the dreaded uppercut. This term refers to a swing that follows an upward arc and often results in a pop fly or a strike. What causes an uppercut swing? When a player tries to pull the bat through the hitting zone with his arms, his rear shoulder droops along with his hands and bat. From this low position, the bat starts its upward path to the ball, and the uppercut is born. Young players have this problem because the proper technique requires more strength and bat control. But they can do it. First, find a lighter bat. Then, work with them on developing quick hip and body rotation along with explosive use of the hands and wrists. The sequence of five hitting drills outlined in chapter 11 is designed to develop these skills, even in young players.

Drills:
- No-Bat Drill **B1**
- Weighted Bat Drill **B2**
- Dry Swings **B3**
- Tee-Hitting **B4**
- Soft Toss **B5**
- Live Hitting **B6**

Swing

Triggered by the inward turning of the rear knee and pushing off of the rear foot, the hips, shoulders, and body rotate explosively and quickly to the pitch. The rear foot pivots, and the hips become square to the pitch. The wrists and hands also snap to the ball. It is crucial that, from the launch position to the point of contact, the shoulders remain level and the hands generate swing speed to hit the ball. Young players who don't have particularly strong forearms tend to pull the bat through the hitting zone with their shoulders and arms and don't use their forearms, wrists, and hands. Often, then, the rear shoulder drops, and the swing follows an upward arc, as opposed to a level path, through the hitting zone. This type of swing is called an *uppercut* and is the most common problem among youth-level and teenage players. That is why it is so important for players to find a bat that is the right size and weight, and also crucial that they get as many swings as possible in practice and at home in order to develop their hitting muscles.

The follow-through: hips rotated, arms continue around the body, good balance.

Follow-through

At contact and in the follow-through, weight should be transferred from the rear foot to an even distribution between both feet. The body continues to uncoil, and the bat arcs around the batter. Players should keep both hands on the bat for control. Lastly, the batter sets the bat down before running—throwing the bat is a common mistake and can injure the catcher or the umpire.

This may seem like a lot of

Stress Individual Goals

When kids are developing their skills at batting and throwing, it is important to stress that they should work toward individual goals. There will always be some players who excel at hitting, and some who don't. You need to be careful that the players who aren't as proficient don't get discouraged because they aren't as good at certain skills as some other players. Rather than challenging your players to excel by saying, "Who can beat the team record with this drill?" make the challenge an individual one. Make sure every player is working toward a personal, realistic goal so that they all feel they are improving—working to accomplish something that is achievable for them.

technique . . . and it is! As a coach, you need to bring your hitters through these mechanical steps in the hitting drills, particularly in the No-Bat Drill (drill B1 on page 141), Weighted Bat Drill (drill B2 on page 141), Dry Swings (drill B3 on page 142), Tee-Hitting (drill B4 on page 142), and Soft-Toss Scrimmage (drill E3 on page 146) outlined in chapters 11 and 12. But as your players develop a swing, don't try to discuss all of these points with each batter. Instead, try to identify one area where each player is having difficulty and help make adjustments within that area. Ingraining all of these fundamental components as muscle memory is an unrealistic goal, but if they can each take away one or two parts of the swing, they will have made great strides. Developing a good hitter's swing takes many years, and you have the opportunity to start them off on the right foot.

Bunting

Bunting is a great way to get all of your hitters, from the most talented to the least, involved and contributing offensively. Regardless of physical strength, experience, or natural ability, all of your players can and *should* learn how to bunt.

Sacrifice Bunting

Players attempt a sacrifice bunt when you, the coach, give the instruction to do so. The intent of this play is to advance a runner one base, either from first base to second or from second base to third, by sacrificing the batter who, in bunting, will most likely be thrown out at first base in a fielder's choice. This is an especially effective play at the youth level because the "easy" play to first base is not so easy for young infielders, and so the sacrifice often results in the runner advancing *and* the batter winding up safe at first. Because the bunt is easier than hitting, it is also a good choice with some hitters who struggle to make contact with the ball.

As the pitcher first begins his windup, the batter assumes the bunting stance, a crucial component of a successful bunt. If he is a right-handed batter, the left foot pivots open, then his right foot moves forward in the batter's box, becomes even with the left foot, and points toward the pitcher. He

Left: The sacrifice bunt: square to the pitcher, weight on the balls of the feet, bat at the top of the strike zone with the barrel end higher than the handle.

Right: The pivot technique, where both feet pivot toward the pitcher, works well when bunting for a hit.

is now square to the pitcher. He then bends his knees and moves his right hand 4 to 5 inches above the grip and, with that hand, pinches the bat. The bat ought to be just below eye level, the barrel slightly higher than the hands, and positioned across the top of the strike zone. For a left-handed batter, the right foot pivots open, then the left leg moves forward in the batter's box, and the left hand moves up on the bat, pinching above the grip, and levels the bat at the top of the strike zone.

Only strikes should be bunted, and because the bat is at the top of the strike zone, any pitch that is above the bat should be called a ball. However, for a player to show that she is not making an attempt to bunt the ball, she must pull the bat back toward her body. Otherwise, it is assumed by the umpire that the player was making an attempt at the pitch and missed, and so a strike is called. Another important rule with regard to bunting is that, with two strikes, a pitch that is bunted foul is ruled strike three, and the batter is called out. Thus, bunting with two strikes is a risky play and is rarely attempted.

The act of bunting is like catching the ball on the bat. The batter needs to "give" with the ball, similar to fielding a ground ball, and deaden it so that it travels only 10 to 20 feet away from the plate. Ideal bunts are laid down the first- or third-base lines, where the play is more difficult for the pitcher or catcher to make.

Drills:

- Bunt-in-a-Bucket `B7`
- Skills Competition `E4`

Bunting for a Hit

Bunting with the intent of getting on base is a more deceptive play in which the batter doesn't square around early but instead pivots his feet toward the pitcher as the ball arrives. He quickly adjusts his hands down the bat to the bunting position, bunts down one of the baselines, and immediately sprints for first base. This is a great skill to teach your faster runners and those players who may struggle making consistent contact with the ball.

Though both right- and left-handed batters can bunt for a hit effectively, lefties have a slight advantage because they are closer to first base to begin with. You may have a lefty who wants to learn to *drag bunt*, where the left-handed batter begins leaning toward first base just as the ball approaches the plate. She then "pulls" or "drags" the bunt down the first-base line. It is a difficult skill, but one that can and should be practiced if any of your "little lefties" want to try it.

Baserunning

Running the bases is a very important aspect of the game, but it generally receives relatively little attention in practice. Anyone who has watched Rickey Henderson run the bases has seen a player who intimidates entire defenses simply by his presence on the base paths. Though he was never the fastest player in the major leagues, he may have been the smartest base runner. Encourage your players by telling them that good baserunning is not dependent upon fast legs but on smart decisions and good habits that each of them can learn.

A good turn: hit the inside corner of the base, lean inside for balance, and swing the arms.

Chapter 9 outlines a progression of drills that introduces the skill of *form running*. I firmly believe that running speed and quickness is the greatest asset an athlete can have in almost any sport. Too often coaches and players think that you either have running speed or you don't—that it's an inherent ability. Certainly there are limitations based on physical makeup and abilities, but running speed can be improved.

Form running is a term that describes proper sprinting technique and includes the action of arms and legs. The progression of drills is designed to isolate each part of the running form and to

Be Alert to Health Problems

There's nothing more frightening for a parent—or coach—than to see a child in distress and not know what to do. Breathing problems, including exercise-induced asthma, are more prevalent in children than ever before. Make sure that you talk to parents about how important it is for you to be aware of any pre-existing physical condition that any of your players may have. In addition, parents need to give you as much information as possible about what to do if their child is in distress, and who to contact if problems occur. Forewarned is forearmed.

Most recreational leagues and schools will have health questionnaires and liability releases. If the league or school doesn't take care of this, getting parents to complete a brief questionnaire should alert you to potential major health issues. Having the league director review the questionnaire before you send it to parents could help make sure you ask all the necessary questions.

Drills:

Form Running:
- Arm Swings   **W1**
- Running in Place   **W2**
- Jog-Sprint   **W3**

Running the Bases:
- Home to First Base   **W4**
- Home to Second Base   **W5**
- First Base to Third   **W6**
- Second Base to Home   **W7**
- Tagging Up   **W8**
- Five-in-One Drill   **W9**

Sliding:
- Bent-Leg Slide   **W10**

practice them individually and then collectively. Practicing this skill is a great way to warm up for practice and prepares your players to run the bases.

Players must become accustomed to the basic rules of baserunning in order to run the bases properly. First of all, rounding the bases is done in a counterclockwise direction. Runners are allowed to overrun first base, as long as they don't commit toward second base, but no other base. Thus, runners need to slide into second, third, and home if there is any threat of being thrown out. I always teach my players this simple rule: "If in doubt, slide." It's the safest and quickest way to approach a base, and it's the best way to avoid being tagged out. Base runners also need to keep an eye out for players ahead of them on the base paths. Two players cannot share the same base, and running past a teammate results in an out. Finally, the base paths are not set routes but instead change depending on whether the base runner is heading directly from one base to another (a straight line) or is rounding a base, in which case the base path is more like an arc. If a player runs outside of this "path" in an attempt to avoid a tag, the base runner is called out.

Depending on the situation, runners want to strike different parts of the base with their feet. For example, a runner trying to beat the throw to first base sprints through the base, landing on the home plate side of the bag. A runner in this situation should never try to slide in to the base unless he is trying to avoid a collision or a tag. Runners who are rounding a base should strike the inside corner of the bag, using it to push off toward the next base. The lead foot on a slide should aim to hit the front and on the outfield side of the base. And when one of your sluggers hits a home run, just make sure she touches every base.

Sliding

There are three reasons to slide into a base: to avoid a tag, to slow or stop at a base, and to avoid a possible collision. To become a good base runner, one must learn how to properly slide.

Minor Injuries? Think RICE

Bumps and bruises are a part of youth sports. If your player's injury needs more attention than the following, be sure to contact your local emergency room or physician. For minor sprains and strains, however, the RICE method will help a minor soft tissue injury heal faster.

- **Relative Rest.** Avoid activities that exacerbate the injury, but continue to move the injured area gently. Early gentle movement promotes healing.

- **Ice.** Apply ice to the affected area for 20 minutes; then leave it off for at least an hour. Do not use ice if you have circulatory problems.

- **Compression.** Compression creates a pressure gradient that reduces swelling and promotes healing. An elastic bandage provides a moderate amount of pressure that will help discourage swelling.

- **Elevation.** Elevation is especially effective when used in conjunction with compression. Elevation provides a pressure gradient: the higher the injured body part is raised, the more fluid is pulled away from the injury site via gravity. Elevate the injury as high above the heart as comfortable. Continue to elevate intermittently until swelling is gone.

The bent-leg slide. Flex the left leg underneath with the right leg flexed to cushion. Keep relaxed and get your hands, head, and arms off the ground.

At the youth level, players should learn the *bent-leg slide* technique. To properly execute this or any type of slide, a player must prepare in time to execute the maneuver. It's common for young players to start their slides too late and find that they jam their feet and legs into the base. Most bases at the youth level are detachable just for this reason, but learning the correct method is still the best defense against injury. The runner should start his slide 6 to 7 feet before the base. The trailing leg becomes the top leg, and the takeoff leg always becomes the underneath bent leg. A player should never jump but should keep his weight low and should glide into the base. The body weight, when hitting the ground, is distributed on the calf, thigh, and buttocks of the bent leg, and the upper body remains relaxed and extended back. The hands, head, and arms are up and off of the ground, and the top leg should be flexed to absorb the impact of the base.

CHAPTER 5

The Practice

Preparation Is Key

The single-most important aspect of a good practice is to *be prepared*. Make sure that you have every minute planned and come to the field with enthusiasm. "Winging it," or planning on setting up the schedule in the few minutes before practice, won't work. Kids will show up to the field early, and you won't have time to put anything together. Preparation will allow you to focus on teaching proper techniques and on your players' development as opposed to worrying about what drill you should do next.

Be Early

Always plan to arrive at least 20 minutes early to practice. You will need to set out the equipment and perhaps move pitching screens, backstops, or other equipment that may have been left on the field by a team that practiced before you. Players, too, will arrive early and may want to practice throwing or work on individual skills. For the first practice, arrive 30 minutes early in preparation for the meeting with parents and kids. This will give you time to introduce yourself and say a little about your hopes and expectations for the season, as well as time to answer their questions.

Get Players to Respond to You Immediately

When you are prepared to begin practice, walk to the edge of the third-base line and call, "Bring it in!" Your players will inevitably take their time gathering around you. You should then let them know how happy you are to see them all and how strong they look as a group, but explain that they've got to learn good team habits right away. When you call, "Bring it in!" they must respond immediately by gathering around you with a spirit of energy and enthusiasm and a willingness to learn and be part of a team. Send them back to where they were when you first called, and tell them to resume exactly what they had been doing. Call "Bring it in!" again, and most likely they will respond with enthusiasm this time. If so, make a big deal of it—tell them: "Great job! You should do that every time!" For more information and advice in establishing good habits, refer to chapter 1, Creating an Atmosphere of Good Habits.

Learn Their Names

The first practice is a very intimidating time for your players. A great way to reduce the tension of these initial moments is to learn their names and involve them in your enthusiasm. The sooner you can learn and begin referring to them by their names, the sooner their confidence in themselves and respect for you will build. Have your players introduce themselves—go around the circle and have each player say his or her name. Explain to them that because you want to learn all of their names that day, you are going to randomly point at kids throughout practice, and they must call out their names. After saying this, look at people in the circle and point your finger indicating that you want them to share their names.

Throughout this first practice, out of the blue just stop what you are doing, point at different players, and learn their names. By doing this, you'll build confidence and self-esteem in your players. Furthermore, this will help in training them to listen to you when you are speaking, and it's a great way to create an immediate bond with your team.

What to Call You

During the first meeting with both parents and kids, let them know what you want to be called—and stick to it. Regardless of the person speaking to you, if it is during a practice or a game, he or she must refer to you by this

Learn your players' names, foster a friendly atmosphere, and you can't go wrong.

name. This policy creates a consistency and establishes your role as team leader. For more advice in this area, see Establish Your Identity as the Coach on page 9.

Explain the Growth Book

Not only will the growth book be a means by which you can keep track of the strengths, weaknesses, and development of each player throughout the season, but it will also be a positive motivator for them. Hold up the book and explain to them that this book will be used to identify each player's respective strengths and areas where work is needed. Explain that throughout the season you'll continually record their individual improvement in the growth book, and that it is with this improvement that you are most concerned. For a more detailed description, see the Growth Book section on page 10.

Format for Practice

Creating a practice environment that fosters improvement, fun, and success is contingent upon a well-organized and well-planned format. This organization is very helpful in establishing a routine for the kids that reinforces good habits. And as your team develops, it will provide a standard by which you can measure and build improvement. You'll need to be flexible to handle the inevitable issues that arise, but these variations shouldn't affect your well-organized and well-established foundation.

The following templates are for two practice sessions. The two-hour session is recommended for 10- to 12-year-olds, and the 90-minute session is designed for 6- to 9-year-olds. These are only suggestions for lengths, and you can adjust the segments according to your needs and available practice time.

Two-hour session

A two-hour session is fine if you include stretching and warm-up. The key is to keep verbiage short and change activity frequently. Work in 15-minute blocks of fielding, base running, throwing drills, etc.
- Team meeting: 5 minutes
- Warm-up/catching and throwing: 10 minutes
- Defensive fundamentals: 30 minutes
- Team defense: 15 minutes
- Batting practice: 40 minutes
- Ending activity—scrimmage situations: 15 minutes
- Wrap-up/recap: 5 minutes

90-minute session
- Team meeting: 5 minutes
- Warm-up/catching and throwing: 10 minutes
- Defensive fundamentals: 15 minutes

Preparation is the single-most important factor in building successful practices. Always plan in advance. A practice worksheet, broken down into the different sequential segments, is an excellent planning tool.

Practice Session Worksheet

Group meeting (5 min.):

_____

_____

_____

_____

Warm-up, catch, and throw (10 min.):

_____

_____

_____

_____

Defensive fundamentals (30 min.):

_____

_____

_____

_____

Team defense (15 min.):

_____

_____

_____

_____

Batting practice (40 min.):

_____

_____

_____

_____

_____

Ending activity: Scrimmage Situations (15 min.):

_____

_____

_____

_____

Wrap-Up/Recap (5 min.):

_____

_____

_____

_____

Practice Session Worksheet

Group meeting (5 min.):

Discuss carpool to Meadville game Wednesday
Go over things we did well against
    Yankees Tuesday
Talk about today's practice.

Warm-up, catch, and throw (10 min.):

Running in place
Home to First-base drill

Defensive fundamentals (30 min.):

Stationary grounders
Forehands and backhands
Knock out, Middle-infield tandem
Batted fly balls

Team defense (15 min.):

Relay drill
Bunt rotation

Batting practice (40 min.):

(split up group) dry swings
            T-hitting
            Live hitting

Ending activity: Scrimmage Situations (15 min.):

Full scrimmage

Wrap-Up/Recap (5 min.):

Team cheer
Mention pizza party following Meadville
    game!

- Team defense: 10 minutes
- Batting practice: 30 minutes
- Ending activity—scrimmage situations: 15 minutes
- Wrap-up/recap: 5 minutes

Team Meeting (5 minutes)

Plan on players getting to the field early. If they don't have particular skills that they want to work on in that extra time, give them something specific to work on. For example, never tell them just to throw the ball. Rather, if they are outfielders, have them work on catching the ball with two hands, or if they are infielders, encourage them to field rolled ground balls concentrating on proper techniques that have been previously taught.

Always begin practice promptly. Call your team in and let them know what specific skills you'll be emphasizing that day and what areas in particular you'll work on. This meeting must be short (5 minutes maximum), lively, and full of anticipation. Always end the meeting with a team cheer of "work hard" and then sprint to the next station.

Warm-Up/Catching and Throwing (10 minutes)

Kids don't take nearly as long as their coaches to warm up their muscles, and they rarely have the discipline to purposefully stretch. Instead, use a fun warm-up activity that actually drills an important skill: base running. Each day you'll work on a different baserunning situation, immediately followed by throwing. In addition to running, this segment of practice focuses on the fundamentals of catching and throwing and provides time for players to loosen up their arms.

Show and tell. The most effective way for a coach to get across a point is by example—demonstrate correct techniques.

The Position Checklist—From the Least to the Most Skilled

Every position on the diamond is important, and there's nowhere that a player can be concealed. In other sports there is always a concern that teammates will avoid passing the ball to a lesser-skilled player, but in baseball when the ball is hit to you or you are at bat, there's nowhere to hide. This is a good thing. But on the other hand, there are positions that are more central to the action. It is important that players get a chance to try all different positions, but don't hesitate to put your highly skilled players at the more skilled positions. The following list organizes the positions from least skilled to most skilled with respect to youth baseball. For example, at higher levels the first baseman is not considered to be one of the more skilled positions, but at the youth level, where catching the ball is still a difficult task, first basemen are placed at a premium.

1. Right field
2. Left field
3. Center field
4. Third base
5. Second base
6. First base
7. Catcher
8. Shortstop
9. Pitcher

Defensive Fundamentals (30 minutes)

Playing defense involves a variety of specific skills, but they are all dependent upon the fundamentals of throwing and catching. Basic practices will involve many drills focused specifically on throwing and catching, but even as you introduce more advanced drills that focus on specific skills—such as fielding ground balls and fly balls, the basics of throwing and catching will constantly be practiced.

The initial step in this process is to determine where each player will play. Most of your players will already designate themselves at a certain position, but you'll need to confirm these designations or change them around depending on the number of kids at each position and their abilities. These positions are not permanent, so don't worry if you decide after the second game that your shortstop would be better suited to playing right field.

Each skill that you teach—from fielding grounders to catching fly balls to proper swing technique—involves a whole set of steps that create a foundation of fundamental mechanics. You'll constantly be looking for things like the proper stance, correct hand and body positioning, proper footwork, fundamental throwing mechanics, two-handed catching, and so forth, and you should emphasize different aspects each practice. But though your job is to introduce these fundamentals, you don't need to continually reinforce all of the steps every chance you get. Give each player one thing to work on at a time. It will take more than one season for these young players to put the whole package together and become complete ballplayers. The practice schedule outlined in the next chapter is designed to foster development, but don't feel that you or your team is a failure if you don't progress upward toward the advanced drills. Spending an entire season on the most basic drills and skills is common and represents the wisest approach you can take if that is what your players need.

Team Defense (10 minutes)

This segment of practice will be the equivalent of your pregame defensive warm-up (see pages 97–98 of chapter 7) in which all of your players will be stationed at their respective positions. From home plate you'll hit balls to the outfield and infield, and this pattern won't change. The drill simulates many different game-like situations, and after your players have been split up into different defensive groups, it's a great way to bring everyone together as a team where they can watch and encourage one another. This segment must be quick and lively with a lot of positive "chatter." Keeping this segment to 10 minutes is key because you are practicing for and simulating the few minutes of defensive preparation that your team is allotted before a game.

Batting Practice (40 minutes)

A common image of batting practice is one player hitting while 14 others stand around watching. This is not an efficient practice! The key to effective batting practice is keeping everyone active, and this is accomplished by organization and purpose.

The following is the format of batting practice, and specifically a rotation of stations, for a 15-player team. At any one time on the actual field of play there ought to be one batter (Live Hitting, drill B6 on page 143), one pitcher (I assume that is you, though a player can also pitch), one feeder (balls hit by the batter are thrown to the feeder, who hands them to the pitcher), and five players busily fielding and shagging the balls hit by the batter. These 7 players are all involved in the Live Hitting component of batting practice. At the same time there are 4 players performing five different batting drills in preparation for Live Hitting. These players are either behind the backstop or somewhere well out the way of the baseballs being hit on the field. They'll need a fence (without pipes) or a screen to hit into for two of the drills. There are also 2 pitchers throwing to 2 catchers on the side and out of the field of play. If you have more than 15 players, add to the number of fielders involved in Live Hitting. If you have fewer than 15, have only 2 or 3 players at a time performing the preparatory hitting drills.

After sending the pitchers and catchers away to throw, assign numbers to the remaining players. Number 1 begins with Live Hitting (give this player some time to warm up and swing a bat, perhaps take a few soft-toss repetitions, and then hit), numbers 2 through 5 begin with the hitting drills, number 6 is the feeder, and numbers 7 through 11 field and shag baseballs. The pitchers and catchers are effectively numbers 12 through 15 and go through the hitting drills and live hitting last.

This leaves no time for complacency and keeps everyone focused on a specific task or skill. During batting practice you, the coach, might be throwing, or instructing the batters, pitchers, and fielders, and keeping the rotation moving quickly. It is very important that you come to understand

Using or Avoiding the Fungo Bat

A fungo bat is a long and skinny piece of equipment that may look more like a curtain rod than a bat. Its shape actually creates a more whip-like feel than a regular bat, and consequently, as a coach, you can generate more power with a lot less effort. Still, you can hit ground balls and fly balls to your fielders with any kind of bat, so don't worry if you don't have an official fungo bat.

But what happens if you have trouble making good contact with this bat? First of all, practice. It may take time, but even coaches improve their skill at hitting practice balls as the season progresses. Secondly, use a toss that feels comfortable to you. Some coaches toss with their right hands and some with their left, and either one is okay as long as your toss is high enough to allow enough time to get both hands on the bat, to get your hands back, and to swing comfortably. Also, make sure that your toss is not too close to your body. Allow for your arms to extend to the baseball. Third, focus on using your hands. Primarily the wrists generate the power in your fungo swing, not your arms and shoulders. Fourth, watch the ball. See it meet the bat. Finally, adjust the arc of your swing for the type of ball you want to hit. In other words, swing slightly downward for a ground ball and slightly upward for a fly ball. But *do not* exaggerate these arc adjustments. If you err in any direction, err to the side of a level swing and effectively increase your margin for error. If you find that your fungo bat seems to have a hole in it, and that hitting the ball is not your particular strength—don't worry. Ask your assistant coach to do the hitting, or recruit a parent to perform the job. If that doesn't work, feel free to throw ground balls and fly balls. There is always a way. Don't let your own difficulties keep you from coaching or even from enjoying the process. After all, you don't have to be able to hit to encourage your players or to create an atmosphere of fun and strong effort.

and know every player's swing and on what area each is working to improve. Be diligent in jotting down notes in your growth book and show your pleasure or satisfaction as you see improvement.

In addition to organization, there are two other crucial components to positive and efficient batting practice: strikes and enthusiasm. The batting practice pitcher, whether it is you, your assistant, or a player, needs to throw a consistent number of strikes. If this becomes difficult, try to get your hands on a pitching screen, move to within 25 feet of the batter, and throw batting practice as if you were tossing darts. In fact, if you have a pitching screen, this is a great and safe way to throw to the players in the Live Hitting drill (drill B6).

The other key component is work habits. Make it a game to keep the rotation flowing quickly from station to station. Offer verbal awards for working up a sweat. Keep the atmosphere focused and fun. If you don't work to create this type of atmosphere, players have a tendency to stand around, talk, and lose focus

Ending Activity: Scrimmage Situations (15 minutes)

This segment is the ending activity and thus should be a competitive and fun time. Your players will have worked on complicated concepts and practiced new skills in the past three segments, so make this time competitive and challenging. Scrimmages or the drill Situations Off Fungo Hits (see drill E1 on page 146 of chapter 12) are an effective way to draw these out. I don't suggest having a Full Scrimmage (drill E3 on page 146) more than once or twice a season because your pitchers may not throw strikes consistently, some kids will have trouble batting, and the time will not be used efficiently. A Soft-Toss Scrimmage (drill E2 on page 146), however, ensures strikes, makes hitting much easier, and results in active play. Kids particularly like scrimmaging because you, the coach, can get involved in the game by pitching to the batter and become part of the fun.

I believe the components of Situations Off Fungo Hits (drill E1) are the best use of this time because you have the power to simulate the exact plays on which you want your team working, and yet it still involves game-like competition, base running, and fun. Mix it up each practice, keep this segment fresh and exciting, and always encourage players to play to win. Create small rewards or consequences for the winning and losing teams, but always in a light-hearted and positive way.

Finally, scrimmages and Situations represent a perfect time to give your field generals chances to practice calling out situations and keeping the defense mentally attuned.

Wrap-Up/Recap (5 minutes)

Always bring your team together again at the end of practice to congratulate them on their hard work and progress that day. Point out specific things they did well as a team and specific players that may have shown exceptional effort or improvement during that practice, as well as areas that need work. *Also, pick something out of practice that they can work on at home to become better players.* This is a good way to get them to practice skills that they find difficult, and it keeps them involved with the game even when they are away from formal practices.

Other Considerations

Flexibility

You won't always be able to include all of these segments—some days you may want to focus more heavily on certain areas. For example, at the beginning of the season, you'll need to spend a bit more time on individual skills, but once the players are used to practice routine, you may only need to briefly review what they have already learned.

Make sure they're listening

Telling your team to listen over and over will never be as effective as actually *training* them to listen to you. Talk to them about the importance of listening to you, explaining that when you are talking you don't want others to be talking, and that you want them to look at you. Then say that you are going to give them a test of their ability to listen. Tell them that when you clap and say, "Everybody up!" they should get up to begin practice, and then explain what you will be doing—running the bases, throwing, and working on infield and outfield drills. Then say, "Everybody up!" but don't clap. Half the team will jump to their feet while you just stand there or yell, "Ah ha!" Let them figure out why some are standing and some are still sitting. Once they all sit back down say, "I guess some of us weren't really listening"; then clap and yell "Everybody up!" and watch them all spring to their feet with their eyes and ears attuned to you. This is an effective way to get your players to realize that when you say you want them to listen to you, you really want them to *hear* what you have to say.

Keep them moving

Kids have incredibly high energy levels and need to be constantly moving. Despite the large number of players on a baseball team and the potential for standing around, particularly during the batting segment of practice, resist it! When explaining a drill, keep their energy levels in mind, make it short, and then let them experiment with the drill. After a few minutes, bring them back in to add further explanation and comment on what they did. Tell them that it is your intent to keep them moving and active and to keep talking at a minimum. Encourage them to make this happen by paying close attention to you when you *do* have to talk.

Scrimmaging

I don't recommend full game type scrimmages in practice except for maybe once or twice in a season. A real scrimmage that includes pitchers on either team takes a long time due to inconsistent pitching and batting. A much more efficient use of time is to have a Soft-Toss Scrimmage (drill E2 on page 146) or set up Situations Off Fungo Hits (drill E1 on page 146). Both of these activities simulate game situations and keep the ball in play for the majority of the time. Plus, they are competitive contests that are fun and rewarding for the kids.

Transition time between practice segments

With the amount of equipment and number of players, transitions during practice, such as moving from defense into batting, can take several minutes. Turn these transitions into a game, and the result will be much more efficient and fun. At the end of a drill such as those in the Team Defense section of chapter 10 (see pages 136–39), let them know that you're almost done and that in a minute you'll need the bats and helmets out, balls to the pitching mound, and players in position. Tell them that world-class speed between drills is 60 seconds, but that they may have trouble being so quick. This will start the competitive juices flowing, and you'll see 15 or so players sprinting around to get things ready. Always offer them praise for their speed and effort, but in a humorous manner challenge them by saying that you think they could be a little bit faster next time.

Encourage politeness and respect

There will be times when you're talking to an individual player, but it is important that your team knows that you are addressing all of them as well. Hence, everyone should be listening and applying what you say to their own skills. A good way to keep the group focused in this way is to insist that they all imitate, or shadow, the skill that you're teaching to a specific individual. This will keep their attention on the game and on their own development.

Players should also know that when you are giving them help with a technique or skill, it is not a two-way conversation. If you say something like, "Billy, you have got to keep your right foot in the batter's box when you square around to bunt. The ump is going to call you out if you don't," he should not engage in a conversation about it—your wish is his command. You are the sole authority figure at practice, and you need to make that clear to every player.

Keep them hydrated

Baseball is played in the hottest months and outside under the sun. It is crucial that you schedule water breaks every 20 to 30 minutes during practice and have water available at the games. Players should be encouraged to bring their own water bottles so as to reduce the lines at the water fountain, but make sure the bottles are labeled with their names. Extreme heat can also be dangerous for young kids, so on very hot days give them a break during practice to sit in the shade and rest.

Help your players to speak up

It's very important that kids are able to use the bathroom if they need to, to sit in the shade if they feel overheated, or to get your attention if they're hurt. Some kids can be very shy with these things. Make a point of addressing these issues at the first practice and let them know that they should speak up if a need arises. Then make sure that you listen. Developing this tone of accessibility is built on trust and approachability. They should feel that when they come to you with a problem or concern, you'll listen respectfully and will be willing to help.

Questions and Answers

Q. We have had only one practice, but we didn't get through even half of the recommended drills and practice segments. What should I focus on if I can't get through the whole thing?

A. Stick with the basics. Don't worry if you don't use even half of the drills in this book. Focus on the segments of the sample practice and work on them until you see real development. The more advanced drills will only frustrate and confuse your players if they don't have a handle on the basics. Most of the drills and activities outlined in this book are easy to learn, but extremely difficult to master. So don't become frustrated. Focus on the fundamentals—catching, throwing, fielding, and batting.

Q. I have had the good luck to get a group of kids that seem to really pick up the skills quickly. We've had two practices, and I've found that the kids are going through the blocks more quickly than the time I've allotted. They are getting bored, and I'm left with a big chunk of time at the end with nothing to do. How should I address this?

A. First of all, make sure that your players are practicing proper fundamentals and not just moving quickly through the drills. Getting through things quickly does not necessarily mean that good habits are forming. If you are satisfied with the direction of their training, transfer the amount of time spent on basic drills to drills and activities performed at various defensive positions. Spend more time practicing the execution of plays in response to game situations through Soft-Toss Scrimmage (drill E2 on page 146) and the Situations Off Fungo Hits drill (drill E1 on page 146). Also, if extra time is available, give each batter in the live hitting station 5 or 10 more swings. Extra time is a gift, not a problem, but make sure you don't short-change proper repetitions of basic fundamentals.

CHAPTER 6

Sample Practices

If you are anything like me, your first practice will get the butterflies moving and set your nerves in motion. But don't be anxious—relax! This chapter outlines in detail a series of practices covering all that you need to do, beginning with the most basic practice and progressing through an intermediate and eventually an advanced session. As players develop their skills in specific areas, and when they display proficiency in a particular drill, they have the opportunity to move from basic to intermediate to advanced drills within that area. Drills are like tests. Once players pass, they can move on to the next one. For instance, you may have one player performing intermediate or advanced ground ball drills while another is still working on the basics. But the same player that is working on ground ball basics might be performing intermediate batting drills. In this way, each player can develop at her own pace without holding back or pressuring other players on the team. Your team also needs to display proficiency with certain team skills before moving to more advanced levels of team play. Keep the information regarding the development of each player private, but encourage each player, no matter what her particular level of skill development.

These sample practices are designed for use as a template for the entire season. They outline the structure of activities, with approximate time allotments for each segment, and cover all aspects of the game. All of the drills listed in this chapter are easy unless otherwise indicated and are described in greater detail in chapters 9 through 12. I have arranged practices at basic, intermediate, and advanced levels, but it is important to realize that you can work different levels of drills within the same practice. Expose your players to the basic progression drills at the beginning of your season, and use them as springboards to the more advanced drills. It is important to realize that most players and teams may never progress beyond these basic skills and drills. If this is the case, don't feel discouraged. Your job is to build a foundation of fundamentals in an atmosphere of fun and good habits, and this takes time.

Basic Beginning Practice

Team Meeting

Your first team meeting should be used to introduce yourself, let your players know what you expect from them, and learn their names (see page 68). At this initial meeting plan to teach or review the fundamentals of throwing, catching, fielding, batting, pitching, and playing catcher and give a brief introduction to team play. And though this is an introductory day, many of the drills used here that teach the fundamentals will remain key parts of every practice throughout the season.

Let the kids know that you appreciate their interest and enthusiasm and that the focus of the day is on the fundamentals of baseball.

Warm-Up/Catching and Throwing

The format for this segment always begins with form running or base running exercises to get the blood flowing. Then players move into catching the ball progression drills and finally into throwing and catching. For the first few practices, the catching progression drills consume some of the time allotted for defensive fundamentals. But, of course, this is the case because playing good defense is impossible without learning the proper fundamentals of catching and throwing.

Form running

The first three drills represent a progression that isolates the various components of sprinting and what I call *form running*.

- **Arm Swings.** This drill isolates the proper action of the arms when sprinting. (See drill W1 on page 118)

- **Running in Place.** This drill adds the proper technique of sprinting on the balls of the feet with the arm action. (See drill W2 on page 118)

- **Jog-Sprint.** This drill puts the arm and leg motion together and allows players to jog in the proper form. The jog then progresses into a sprint. (See drill W3 on page 118)

Catching and Throwing

- **Above, below, and at the Waist.** This is a progression of drills that works on proper fundamentals of catching a ball that is thrown above, below, or at the waist. The progression begins using no ball and then moves to using an Incredi-ball (or tennis balls if you don't have Incredi-balls) and finally a baseball. The purpose of this progression is for players to develop confidence and learn how to position themselves for a catch. By using no ball, kids have no fear of being hit and can focus on technique. Once the

The Glove-Side Drill and Throwing-Side Drill emphasize stance and ready hands.

technique has been practiced, incorporate the softer Incredi-ball. This stage of the progression will build players' confidence in their techniques and will prepare them for the final step of using the hardball. (See drill W11 on page 122)

- **Glove-Side Drill** and **Throwing-Side Drill.** Both these drills follow the same progression as the previous drill, but they simulate catching throws to the player's right and left. (See drill W12 and drill W13 on page 123)

- **Five Every Five.** This drill gives your players a chance to practice proper throwing mechanics and to practice the catching skills learned in the previous drills. (See drill W15 on page 124)

- **Focus Drill.** Players begin concentrating on throwing to a specific target using the proper throwing fundamentals. This drill is performed as a part of Five Every Five. (See drill W15 and drill W16 on page 124)

Defensive Fundamentals

Most often the infield and outfield separate during this segment—you can work with one group, and your assistant coach can work with the other. These basic drills continue to focus on catching and throwing, often by using progression drills, but they also introduce the techniques of fielding ground balls and fly balls. Early in the season you will still be evaluating positions and moving players around as you come to know their respective strengths and weaknesses.

Infield

- **Ground Ball Work.** This progression drill should begin every infield session. It breaks down each component of fielding different types of ground balls, including preparation, stance, and hands, using easy, hand-delivered rollers. You needn't use the Forehands and Backhands stage of the progression in the basic practices.(See drill D1 on page 125)

- **All at Shortstop.** This drill gets players comfortable with seeing and fielding the ball off of the bat. (See drill D5 on pages 126–27)

- **Knockout.** This game introduces a competitive element and rewards the discipline of squaring up to the ball. (See drill D7 on page 127) (easy–intermediate)

Outfield

- **Wave Drill without Ball.** This is a progression drill that works on first step, footwork, and using two hands. Once again, by using no ball players aren't afraid of being hit and thus can concentrate on executing proper technique. (See drill D15 on pages 131–33)

- **Wave Drill with Ball.** This is similar to the previous drill except it incorporates using a thrown baseball. (See drill D16 on pages 133–34) (easy–intermediate)

- **Outfielder's Ground Ball Techniques (without Ball).** This drill works specifically on making three types of fielding plays on outfield grounders. (See drill D18 on pages 134–35)

- **Outfielder's Ground Ball Techniques with Ball.** This is similar to the previous drill except it incorporates batted or thrown ground balls. (See drill D19 on page 135)

Team Defense

There is *no team defense* for the first practice and until your players are comfortable with the routine of the progression drills. At that point your players will be ready to work on team defense.

Batting Practice

As mentioned in chapter 5, good batting practice is accomplished through organization of the station rotation, throwing consistent strikes, and a focused and controlled atmosphere. It is important to note that the most significant progress with the fundamentals of batting is made through concerted effort in the five main hitting drills: No-Bat Drill, Weighted Bat Drill, Dry Swings, Tee-Hitting, and Soft Toss. Even if live hitting is too advanced for some, all of your players, from the most skilled to the least, will experience the satisfaction of hitting a baseball in these drills.

Batting

The following drills are to be practiced in sequence and done in preparation for Live Hitting. The intent of these drills is to teach the fundamentals, to work on various swing locations, and to develop the swing instinct or "muscle memory"—that which one has practiced over and over. During games a batter should be thinking only about hitting the ball, but practice is the time to drill the technique and get a lot of proper repetitions.

- **No-Bat Drill.** This drill takes the bat out of the equation and helps players practice four of the five fundamental components of the swing—stance, stride, launch position, and swing—and even the visual approach. (See drill B1 on page 141)

- **Weighted Bat Drill.** This drill helps to build wrist and arm strength while maintaining proper swing fundamentals. It also prepares the batter for the next drill. (See drill B2 on page 141)

- **Dry Swings.** Players practice their swing techniques while swinging at four different pitches pictured in their minds; high, low, inside, outside. After swinging the weighted bat, the regular bat feels light and is fun to swing. This drill incorporates grip, stance, cocking action, stride, and a good level swing. (See drill B3 on page 142)

A batting tee can help with hitting fundamentals. Even major league hitters use batting tees daily.

- **Tee-Hitting.** Working with a partner, each batter swings at a stationary ball set on a batting tee in the four different pitch locations. They hit the baseballs into a net, fence, or screen. (See drill B4 on page 142)

- **Soft Toss.** Here players use the same swing, except now the ball is moving toward the batter. Tossers should focus primarily on tossing pitches in the middle of the plate. Again players work in pairs and hit into a net, fence, or screen. (See drill B5 on page 143) (easy–intermediate)

- **Live Hitting.** Players bat against the pitcher and try to continue to use the swing they have developed in the preceding drills. Each batter gets a total of 10 to 12 swings. (See drill B6 on page 143) (intermediate)

Pitching

- **Fives Drill.** Pitchers throw to catchers who set up in five different locations relative to the plate—on both corners and in the middle plus high and low. The drill emphasizes proper pitching fundamentals and throwing accuracy and helps to build arm strength and to ingrain proper and consistent mechanics. (See drill B8 on pages 144–45)

Playing Catcher

- **Fives Drill.** As pitchers throw, catchers get sufficient work catching in full equipment. (See drill B8 on pages 144–45)

- **Blocking the Ball Drill.** This drill works on the basics of blocking pitches thrown in the dirt. (See drill B9 on page 145)

Ending Activity: Scrimmage Situations

- **Soft-Toss Scrimmage.** This segment is meant to be a fun-filled and competitive activity. As mentioned in chapter 5, full scrimmages are rarely a good idea, but situational work involving soft tosses are a great use of time and lots of fun. In this fun scrimmage, everyone gets a chance to hit and a chance to field, and you can play, too. After your team has played a game, however, and you have some specific game situations to work on, end with the Situations Off Fungo Hits drill. (See drill E1 on page 146)

Wrap-Up/Recap

Bring your players into a huddle and tell them that you are very pleased with their efforts and, if it's the first practice, that you're excited for the season to start. Reassure them that the next practice will move faster and they will be learning new techniques each day. Encourage them all to practice the techniques learned at home, and then announce the time and place of the next meeting. End with a cheer: "One, two, three, TEAM!"

This template for a basic session is not necessarily designed so that you can fit in all of these drills and get all these techniques across during your early practices. Understanding and practicing the basic fundamentals of the game will take up the majority of your time. Be patient. Use this basic design for as many practices as necessary, and remember that, within this system, teammates can develop side by side and at their own pace. Also, evaluate the needs of your team—if players need more time in a certain area, make the necessary scheduling adjustments. Conversely, if they are progressing quickly through the basics, spend more time doing group work and situations.

Intermediate Practice

Team Meeting

This time when you meet with your players, challenge them to pay special attention to some new skills such as the forehand and backhand fielding techniques, on defense or in hitting, developing a rhythm to get their hands back in the launch position to swing. Have the players understand they are building on the basic fundamentals they have already learned and practiced.

Warm-Up/Catching and Throwing

You should know all of your players' names by now, so make a game of it. As they run the bases in the warm-up phase, call out each player's name as he or she begins the sprint to first base.

Form Running

Have a quick run-through of the three form-running drills.

- **Arm Swings** (See drill W1 on page 118)

- **Running in Place** (See drill W2 on page 118)

- **Jog-Sprint** (See drill W3 on page 118)

   Then move your players immediately into baserunning drills.

- **Home to First Base.** Players sprint from home plate to first base making sure to run through the base and then to veer off into foul territory. (See drill W4 on page 119)

- **Home to Second Base.** Sprinting from home plate to second base, players work on rounding first plate and striking the inside portion of the base. (See drill W5 on page 119)

- **Second Base to Home.** Players sprint from second base to home plate and work on properly rounding third base. (See drill W7 on page 120)

Catching and Throwing

- **Catching the Ball Drill.** Work more quickly through the steps as your players become more accustomed to the routine, but don't sacrifice proper technique. (See drill W11 on pages 122–23)

- **Ball to Glove-Side Drill.** Again, work quickly through the routine. (See drill W12 on page 123)

- **Backhand Drill.** This drill follows the format of the previous two drills but works on catching balls thrown to the far backhand side of the body. (See drill W14 on pages 123–24)

- **Five Every Five.** Players should try to increase the maximum distance at which they throw by a few feet each practice, unless they feel soreness or cannot make accurate throws. (See drill W15 on page 124)

- **Focus Drill.** (See drill W16 on page 124)

Defensive Fundamentals

Continue to focus on the fundamentals of infield and outfield throwing and catching, but within the context of more advanced drills.

Infield

- **Ground Ball Work.** Emphasize previous fundamentals, but add the challenge of increasing quickness. Also add to Direct Ground Balls and Side-to-Side Ground Balls the Forehands and Backhands drill. (See drills D1, D2, D3, and D4 on pages x125–26) (easy–intermediate)

- **All at Shortstop.** This time, emphasize moving forward on the ball and playing the big hop. Play the ball; don't let the ball play you. (See drill D5 on pages 126–27)

- **Field and Throw.** This drill incorporates the throw to first base. This can be off rolled ground balls or short fungoes. (See D6 on page 127) (easy–intermediate)

- **Ground Balls at Positions.** Players field ground balls from their respective positions and make the throw to first base. The coach moves around the infield about 50 feet away from each fielder. (See drill D12 on pages 130–31) (easy–intermediate)

- **Bobbled Balls.** From their positions, players simulate a bobbled ball situation and work on picking the baseball up with the two hands, getting their feet under control, and throwing accurately to first base. (See drill D13 on page131)

- **Slow Rollers to Third Base.** At the same time as the players perform the Middle-Infield Double Play Drill, players at third base charge slowly rolling ground balls and throw to first base. (See drill D9 on page 128) (intermediate)

- **Middle-Infield Double Play Drill.** At the same time as the players perform the Slow Rollers to Third Base drill, players at second base and shortstop work on fielding hand-rolled ground balls and making the feed and force out at second base. (See drill D10 on pages 128–29)

Outfield
- **Wave Drill without Ball.** Emphasize taking a proper angle to the ball. (See drill D15 on pages 131–33)

- **Wave Drill with Ball.** Use thrown fly balls for accuracy. (See drill D16 on pages 133–34) (easy–intermediate)

- **Batted Fly Balls.** This drill allows players to see fly balls off a bat for the first time. Many balls will be misjudged, but that is okay. For players who seem comfortable catching, encourage them to work on making crow-hops into the throwing position. (See drill D20 on page 135) (intermediate)

Team Defense

This will be the first time that your whole team is assembled together as a defense. Keep the attitude positive and expect mistakes. Don't do much teaching during the Infield Practice section, but instead have players focus on the format of the drill. This will become your pregame defensive routine.

- **Relay Drill.** This game-drill focuses on the relay throws made from the outfield to the infield and rewards accuracy and quickness. (See drill D22 on pages 136–37)

- **Infield Practice.** All players assume their defensive positions, and a routine of fly balls and ground balls hit to the outfield and infield is established. Emphasize again the day's challenge: making accurate throws. (See drill D25 on pages 139–40) (easy–intermediate)

- **Covering on a Steal.** Coverage drills are more advanced but must be covered and practiced. This drill directly uses only the second basemen, shortstops, and catchers, but the remaining infielders should stay alert, calling out "He's going" when the base runner steals. Any players who are not on defense can act as the base stealers. Because this drill is done at the end of Infield Practice, outfielders are already in center field catching batted fly balls. (See drill D24 on pages 137–39) (intermediate)

Batting Practice

Batting

The emphasis at this practice is on developing a cocking action, getting the hands back into a good launch position, and watching the ball. This doesn't mean that you should neglect the specific areas on which individual batters need work. But because you won't be able to work with every player, it is helpful to have something on which each can focus. At this age, always emphasize keeping the eyes on the ball. They should visually track the pitch right to the bat.

- **No-Bat Drill.** (See drill B1 on page 141)

- **Weighted Bat Drill.** (See drill B2 on page 141)

- **Dry Swings.** (See drill B3 on page 142)

- **Tee-Hitting.** (See drill B4 on page 142)

- **Soft Toss.** Players can begin working more intently on hitting balls tossed to inside and outside locations. (See drill B5 on page 143) (easy–intermediate)

- **Live Hitting.** (See drill B6 on page 143) (intermediate)

Pitching

- **Fives Drill.** In each set of five pitches, the pitcher attempts to improve accuracy and power using a basic and efficient motion. (See drill B8 on pages 144–45)

Playing Catcher

- **Fives Drill.** (See drill B8 on pages 144–45)

- **Blocking the Ball Drill.** (See drill B9 on page 145)

Ending Activity: Scrimmages and Situations

- **Situations.** After you have played at least one game, you'll remember certain situations that gave your team difficulties. Position nine players on defense and use the remaining players as base runners. Then simply set up the identical situations that you faced in the game and hit fungoes to the defense to control the situations. This is a great way to instruct your team and to get everyone involved in a fun activity that includes defense, base running, and teamwork. (See drill E1 on page 146)

Wrap-Up/Recap

Bring your players in and congratulate them for a good practice and a willingness to work toward improvement. Depending on what didn't go so well during practice, give them something to work on at home. Finally, announce the next practice or game and end with a team cheer.

Advanced Practice

Team Meeting

This time when you meet with your team, let them know they will be working on more advanced skills such as double play pivots, bunt coverage, etc. During batting practice, the emphasis could be on developing more swing speed by using better trunk rotation, yet not pulling the head and shoulders off the ball.

Warm-Up/Catching and Throwing

- **Home to First Base.** (See drill W4 on page 119)

- **Bent-Leg Slide.** Players learn and work on the proper sliding technique. (See drill W10 on pages 121–22)

- **First Base to Third Base.** Players sprint from first base to third base, work on rounding second base, and slide into third. (See drill W6 on pages 119–20)

- **Tagging Up.** Players practice tagging up on a fly ball from third base to home. (See drill W8 on page 120)

- **Five-in-One Drill.** In this drill, players practice five different baserunning situations at one time. (See drill W9 on pages 120–21)

Catching and Throwing

- **Five Every Five.** Players continue to increase the throwing distance between partners. (See drill W15 on page 124)

- **Focus Drill.** (See drill W16 on page 124)

- **Quick Drill.** Throwing partners work on making short and accurate throws as quickly as possible for 30 seconds. This drill ends the Five Every Five drill. (See drill W17 on page 124)

Defensive Fundamentals

Infield

- **Ground Ball Work.** Build on the fundamentals that players have already learned and add various throwing techniques such as the underhand toss back to one's partner. (See drill D1 on page 125) (easy–intermediate)

- **Hot Potato.** In this drill, emphasize the punch throw, quick ball exchange, and the use of two hands in catching. (See drill D8 on pages 127–28) (intermediate)

- **Field and Throw Off Short Fungoes.** Emphasize gliding through the ball and making strong accurate throws to first, or feeds to second base. (See drill D6 on page 127) (easy–intermediate)

- **Slow Rollers to Third Base.** (See drill D9 on page 128) (intermediate)

- **Middle-Infield Double Play Drill.** (See drill D10 on pages 128–29) (intermediate)

- **Turning Double Plays.** Middle infielders go from just making the force-out in the Tandem Drill to turning double plays. This is a very difficult drill, and you may decide to never attempt it with your players. (See drill D11 on pages 129–30) (advanced)

- **Dive Drill.** In this drill, players practice getting quickly to their feet after making a diving stop to either the forehand or backhand, and making an accurate throw. (See drill D14 on page 131)

Outfield:
- **Outfielder's Ground Ball Techniques (without Ball).** (See drill D18 on pages 134–35)

- **Outfielder's Ground Ball Techniques with Ball.** (See drill D19 on page 135) (easy–intermediate)

- **Quarterback Drill.** This game-drill works on running catches. (See drill D17 on pages 134–35) (intermediate)

- **Batted Fly Balls**. (See drill D20 on page 135) (intermediate)

- **Communication Drill.** This drill focuses on communication between outfielders on fly balls and ground balls. Players practice calling for the ball, reducing the chance of players colliding in the outfield. You can either throw or hit these fly balls. (See drill D21 on page 135) (intermediate)

Team Defense
- **Defensive Coverage on Various Batted Balls.** Continue to work on establishing the routine of the drill. Emphasize hitting the cut-off man and throwing to the proper base. (See drill D25 on pages 139–40)

- **Bunt Rotation.** Like Covering on a Steal, this drill involves more of you talking and players listening than most drills. Use back-up infielders as runners. Outfielders catch batted fly balls in center field during this drill. (See drill D23 on page 137) (intermediate)

- **Bunt-in-a-Bucket.** While you have the whole team together, players compete in this game-drill that works on bunting accuracy and uses the square-around sacrifice bunt technique. (See drill B7 on page 144)

Batting Practice

Batting

These drills emphasize a quick and explosive rotation of the rear knee, hips, and shoulders as the way to generate power. Remind players that by using the body to generate bat swing, they will hit the ball harder and farther. Daily, emphasize a good level swing.

- **No-Bat Drill.** (See drill B1 on page 141)

- **Weighted Bat Drill.** (See drill B2 on page 141)

- **Dry Swings.** (See drill B3 on page 142)

- **Tee-Hitting.** (See drill B4 on page 142)

- **Soft Toss.** Include quicker tosses that simulate fastballs and that force the batter to be more aggressive and quicker with the hips. (See drill B5 on page 143) (easy–intermediate)

- **Live Hitting.** (See drill B6 on page 143) (intermediate)

Pitching

- **Fives Drill.** (See drill B8 on pages 144–45)

Playing Catcher

- **Fives Drill.** (See drill B8 on pages 144–45)

- **Blocking the Ball Drill.** (See drill B9 on page 145)

Ending Activity: Scrimmage Situations

- **Skills Competition.** Once or twice per season, instead of a Soft-Toss Scrimmage (drill E2 on page 146) or Situations Off Fungo Hits (drill E1 on page 146), have a skills competition including tests of throwing accuracy, fielding proficiency, and making consistent batting contact. Have one skills competition toward the beginning of the season and one toward the end. Record the results in the growth book and take note of each player's progress. (See drill E4 on page 147)

Wrap-Up/Recap

Bring your team in and tell them how pleased you are with the progress they have made and their hard work. If they have been winning a lot of games, warn them not to become complacent but to maintain their hard work in practice and their energetic, fun spirit on the field. If they have been losing, let them know that baseball is a tough game to learn, and a real challenge. Encourage them not to give up—keep up the hard work and good things will happen. Tell them again how proud you are of them, and end with a cheer.

Questions and Answers

Q. No one on my team, including myself, can throw strikes, and we can't afford a pitching screen. Batting practice is taking over an hour, and kids are standing around. What should I do?

A. Kids must not be left standing around! The first thing to do is to make sure that there isn't someone on your team who can throw strikes. If this is actually the case, you need to do two things. First, have players and your assistant coach throw 12–15 pitches to each batter and treat it as if your team were facing an inaccurate pitcher. Have your players swing only at strikes, but cut off each player's turn at 15 pitches, regardless of the number of strikes thrown. Use more tee and soft toss drills to get the players a lot of swings. This is where the primary batting development will take place, and you should treat these drills as the focal point of batting practice. The second thing to do is to seek out a batting practice pitcher. Either call or send home a letter stating your need for someone who can fill this role. Let them know how important this job is and that any help would be greatly appreciated. You can also ask the school athletic director or a coach of older kids if they would have a player who could come throw strikes to your team once or twice per week. Finding someone who can keep things moving and throw a steady diet of strikes is key to a fun and beneficial practice.

Q. I have eight kids who want to play shortstop. I want my players to play where they are excited to play, but clearly all of them can't play the same position. What should I do?

A. Explain to them that only one player can field the shortstop position at one time, and that each one of them *will* have the opportunity to do just that. Describe the substitution schedule to them, pointing out that each one of them will most likely have the chance to play shortstop for at least one inning every game. Also tell them that they will find themselves at a variety of other positions throughout the season and that, as a complete ballplayer, they need to learn how to play at those other spots. During practice, encourage these kids when they make plays at other positions. Boost their confidence and interest in other positions through positive reinforcement. For example, you might call out during an outfield drill: "Great job using two hands, Billy. That's the way to play a solid right field!" Cultivate their interest in the shortstop position, but maintain a positive team attitude as you spread your players to all nine positions.

Q. I made it clear that I expected my players to respect the umpires and their decisions, but the ump we had at the first game was terrible and clearly didn't know some of the rules of the game. I didn't say anything at the time, but after the game my players had questions about the rules and the umpire. What do I tell them?

A. You will not always be pleased with the umpiring, but it's very important that your players know that they are not to question calls. They should understand that just as they make mistakes in the field and at the plate, so too will umpires make mistakes from time to time. Challenge them with the fact that a respectful ball club never disputes a call but instead respects the umpire's decision and focuses on their job—the next pitch or the next play. Let them know that they did a good job of this, that you were proud to represent such a classy group of ballplayers, and that by the end of the season, in addition to solid play, you hope that your team will be known for its sportsmanship.

Q. We won our first game, and after it was over some of my players were whooping and shouting. I was glad they were excited, but how much celebrating after a win is too much?

A. It's terrific to be happy after a win, but it's also important to represent good sportsmanship to your opponents. Get your kids into a huddle, congratulate them on a well-played game, and remind them of the other team and how it feels to lose. Encourage them to show respect for the other players and for their efforts on the field by not "whooping it up." Keep it low-key after the game, and as a team, be consistent with the huddle and with the sportsmanlike behavior.

Q. Our team lost in a huge way. The kids worked hard and played well, but we were simply outmatched. Now they're feeling very low. How can I get them back on track and excited again?

A. Immediately after the game, let them know how proud you are of their effort and their willingness to work at the game. Point out that their opponents have a very good team, a lot of good players, and they play the game right. That's the way we want to play in the future. Encourage them to keep striving for improvement in practice. When the next practice comes along, incorporate specific drills and game-like situations into the mix. Emphasize what they are doing right, and keep the atmosphere light and full of activity. Without realizing it, they'll forget about the disappointment incurred by a losing streak and will be caught up in the fun of the game.

CHAPTER 7

Game Time

The Mental Aspect

Regardless of how many years you have participated in sports, you'll never get rid of the nervous pregame jitters that creep in right before the first pitch of the season. You've worked hard in the preseason, and this may seem like a real test of your preparation and ability as a coach. It's easy to get caught up in the excitement of every strike, every base hit, and every run that's scored, and it's tempting to judge your success by what the scoreboard reads at the end of the game. Remember, however, that the only guarantee in this game is that one team will win and another will lose—and you need to prepare yourself to accept either with grace and a sense of humor. Each game is an opportunity for the kids to display skills and sportsmanship and to discern areas of strength and weakness.

Make sure your players stay in the game mentally and are supportive of their teammates.

Set an Example

The most important role you'll play on the field and in front of your players is the example they see. The example they should see is one of support and encouragement toward your players and one of control and respect toward umpires, the opposing team, and the game's situations. Striving to win should be an objective, but it should never supersede fairness and sportsmanship on your part. No matter how much you talk to your players about these objectives, what you do, particularly in the heat of the battle, will speak most loudly about what you believe.

Respect the Umpires

Baseball offers ample time before games to meet the umpires, whether they are paid professionals, volunteer parents, or high school kids. Shake their hands and offer them the respect they deserve. Once the game begins, if you disagree with an ump's call, forget about it and concentrate on your role as being a positive role model and teacher to the players. If an umpire

makes a mistake, immediately give your players something to do before they have time to dwell on the call. Tell them to make the next play and to concentrate on the game situation. Because of the antics we often see from coaches on TV and in youth games across the country, this is a wonderful area in which you can stand out as an example of proper coaching behavior.

Umpires are going to make mistakes—just as surely as you and your players will. The real issue is how you respond when the umpires do blow a call. If you let a bad call adversely affect you, your team will

Umpires have a tough job. Teach your players to respect their calls, effort, and commitment.

notice and they, in turn, will be affected. Constantly remind yourself that as the coach your role is to be a model of sportsmanship and a positive spirit. If you can respond to a bad call with this in mind, you'll have real clout behind your words when you instruct your players not to question an umpire's call.

At the end of the game, no matter the outcome or the umpire's performance, greet him or her with a handshake and a thank-you. Most often, your umpires will be volunteers, but regardless, they deserve your thanks and respect.

Players Who Misbehave

Explain to your players before the first game that they are part of a classy team that is respectful of one another, of umpires, and of the opposing team. This means that any physical signs of argument with an umpire's call, such as pounding a bat or rolling their heads, are unacceptable. It also means that jeering the other team's player or in any way embarrassing an opponent are signs of poor sportsmanship and will not be tolerated on our team. If they do behave disrespectfully, let them know that you will disci-

Scoring Position

If you listen to a baseball announcer on TV or the radio, or if you hang around coaches for very long, you might hear someone say something about "runners in scoring position." What are they talking about? Obviously, anyone who is on base or even at bat is in scoring position, meaning they have the potential of scoring at any moment. But when people refer to runners in scoring position they mean that the runners are capable of scoring on a single. The players who are within range of scoring should a single be hit are those who are on either second or third base.

pline them. This does not mean that you should make a public spectacle of the situation and humiliate the kid out on the field, but you definitely need to communicate to the player on the bench a clear and prompt message that such behavior will not be tolerated. In extreme situations or if the player is a "repeat offender," take him out of the game after that half-inning. Always make sure, however, that you let the player know that he should learn from this bad experience and you know it won't happen again.

Be Prepared

Just as you need to be ready for practice, you need to have a game plan established before you show up at the field. Your game plan will include having the necessary equipment, the pregame practice routine, the starting lineup, and a substitution schedule. You should also decide beforehand what you will do if you are winning by a lot, losing by a lot, or caught in a close game. The kids will be excited—you will need to be in control and be ready with a full pregame schedule that focuses their energy.

Make sure, before you leave your home, that all of the equipment is accounted for, including the first-aid kit. The home team usually furnishes game balls, but make sure that you have a few good ones in your bag just in case.

Have 6- to 9-year-olds arrive 20 minutes before game time. This allows for a few short drills that work on fundamentals, and then they're ready to start the game. Pregame drills ought to consist of

- Jog to the foul pole and back as a team
- Five Every Five (see drill W15 on page 124)
- Ground balls for infielders and thrown fly balls for outfielders (done simultaneously) (see drill D1 on page 125)
- Pitcher warms up with catcher; Dry Swings for everyone else (done simultaneously) (see drill B3 on page 142)

Have 10- to 12-year-olds arrive 45 minutes before game time in order to work on a few short drills and to run through the Team Defense drills. Both teams will get 10 to 15 minutes to use the field before the game.

While your team is on the field, they can warm up with these drills:

- Jog to the foul pole and back as a team
- Five Every Five (See drill W15 on page 124)
- Team Defense drills (see drills D22, D23, D24, and D25 on pages 136–40)
- Infield Practice (See drill D25 on pages 139–40)

In the last drill, Infield Practice, outfielders throw to second base, third base, and home. (In the interest of time, outfielders could throw just to second base.) Infielders can go through the entire routine including double plays.

During the other team's time on the field, have your players do the following drills off the field:

- Ground Ball Work (See drill D1 on page 125)
- Tee Drills
- Soft Toss Drills
- Fives Drill (pitcher and catcher) (See drill B8 on page 144)
- Dry Swings (See drill B3 on page 142)

Explain Your Substitution Pattern

The substitution schedule is an important issue, so you should plan it out ahead of time. Once a player is taken out of the game, he or she may or may not be allowed to come back in depending on league rules. Though to some extent it is unavoidable, you should not rotate players through different positions within the same game. It is important, particularly for the 6- to 9-year-olds, that players be exposed to different positions, but they also need to gain a real feel for playing the same position for an entire game. So for this age group you should rotate the players' positions each game but try to keep them at the same position during the game. Pitchers and catchers will be on their own rotation pattern because not all players will want or be able to play these positions. Make sure that in each game the pitching and catching duties are split evenly. As for the remaining seven field players, most of them will split the game with another teammate at the same position, resulting in each kid playing three innings apiece. Don't worry if one or more players get to play the entire game while others are playing only half, but make sure that this privilege of playing the whole game is also on a rotating schedule.

It is possible that, even at these younger ages, your players will develop affinities for specific positions, and you may want to keep them there game after game. Whether or not this happens at the 6- to 9-year-old level, the majority of the players on a team of 10- to 12-year-olds ought to play the entire season at one *or two* positions. There will be exceptions

Running It Out

As a coach, you want to instill in your players an attitude of hard work and good hustle. One of the most obvious signs of a team that has been coached to work hard and to hustle is one that sprints all-out after hitting a ball. Don't let your players adopt the habits of many major leaguers who are often guilty of jogging to first base after grounding the ball to an infielder. Your players should sprint through first base, regardless of where the ball is hit. No play should be assumed an automatic out, for good things happen to those who hustle. The same goes for fly balls. If the ball is hit high in the air, challenge your players to sprint for second base just in case the ball is dropped. What a joy it is to see young players playing the game with energy and respect. Congratulate them for their hustle and self-discipline and let them know how good it looks.

to this on every team, most notably with regard to the pitcher, who will be able to pitch just once per week and who thus must play another position. But for the most part, you should divide playing time by position.

You should flip-flop the players who start and the players who finish each game so that the same kids don't always play the first three innings or the last three innings of every contest. Also, try to arrange combinations of players that will work well together. You will always want to have a field general in the game who will keep the other players aware of the situations. In general, you want to have your strongest players "up the middle"—meaning at catcher, pitcher, shortstop, second base, and center field—and at first base. Obviously, this will not always be possible, but playing your more skilled players at these positions often makes a very difficult game progress more smoothly for everyone on the field. Trying to be perfectly equitable by evenly distributing players at all positions can produce unnecessary frustration for everyone involved. For example, imagine a ground ball that is hit to the third baseman, a player who often struggles with successfully fielding the ball *and* making an accurate throw. He then fields the grounder and throws to first base—on-line, but a bit too low. To mishandle the throw would negate the fine fielding play and would probably make the third baseman forget about what he had done well. But if the first baseman manages a difficult catch, and the runner is called out, the third baseman, instead of feeling dejected because of yet another error, is elated and develops confidence for the next play. By strategically placing skilled players in a few of these positions, the game can be more fun and a better learning experience for your entire team. However, don't confine players to certain positions if they have aspirations to play elsewhere. Give them the opportunity to play a variety of positions.

In general, and above all else, it is important that you distribute equal playing time to your players. Perfect division of innings is not possible, but preparing a substitution schedule in advance is the best way to reward players for their efforts and commitment to the team.

The substitution patterns I describe are designed for a team of 15 players. Certain leagues abide by the *closed substitution* rule, which means that players who leave the game are not allowed to reenter, as opposed to *free substitution*, which allows reentry. If there is closed substitution (more common among 10- to 12- year-old leagues), at the start of the fourth inning, substitute the six players on the bench for six players in the game. This leaves three positions in which there is no need for substitution. Either switch players around to different positions or keep these three players where they are. Just make sure, for each new game, that you rotate the three players who get to play all six innings.

If your league allows free substitution, arrange your substitution pattern according to the schedule shown below. Modify it according to the number of players on your team and according to certain pitching demands that you may have (that is, players who cannot pitch can "skip over" the pitching slot in the schedule).

Substitution Pattern for a team of 15 players (columns represent positions and rows represent innings)

	Positions									Substitutes					
	P	C	1b	2b	3b	SS	LF	CF	RF	A	B	C	D	E	F
1st	1	2	3	4	5	6	7	8	9	10	11	12	13	14	15
2nd	10	11	12	13	14	15	1	2	3	4	5	6	7	8	9
3rd	4	5	6	7	8	9	10	11	12	13	14	15	1	2	3
4th	13	14	15	1	2	3	4	5	6	7	8	9	10	11	12
5th	7	8	9	10	11	12	13	14	15	1	2	3	4	5	6
6th	1	2	3	4	5	6	7	8	9	10	11	12	13	14	15

In addition to specifying each player's position each inning, you can also assign specific jobs to each substitute every inning. For example, substitute A chases foul balls; B arranges the helmets and bats and keeps them out of play; C coaches first base; and D, E, and F must maintain consistent chatter.

Batting Order

You also need to establish a batting order for each game that allows players to hit in different spots in the lineup each game. Very simply, you can use the position numbers—1 through 9—to create this rotating pattern. For the first game, bat through the order from 1 to 9 or, in other words, from the pitcher to the right fielder. Begin the second game with 9, 1, 2, 3, . . . and the third game with 8, 9, 1, 2, 3, . . . Then, when you substitute for a player, the new player will simply fill in the appropriate spot in the batting order.

Meet the Other Coach and the Umpires

Take time before the game to shake hands and introduce yourself to the opposing coach and the umpires. It's amazing how quickly simple gestures like a handshake, a smile, and a few friendly words will dissolve any potential for misunderstanding later. When you think about it, you're all in this for the same purpose, letting the kids enjoy the game and have fun. Be sure to ask the umpires to go over any ground rules (exceptions or special circumstances specific to the ballfield, such as "a ball is foul if it hits the branches overhanging the foul line in right field"). You'll be glad you did if something unusual happens during the game.

Coaching the Game
The Start of the Game

After you meet with the opposing coach, bring your team in, offer a few words of encouragement and inspiration, remind them to have fun and to be respectful, and urge them to play hard. Have a team cheer: "One, two, three, team!" and then, if you're the home team and are starting on defense, players who are in the game should sprint to their positions, eager to play, while the rest of the players should sit on the bench. If you begin on offense, your first batter should put on a helmet and head toward the plate, while the on-deck batter warms up by running through a shortened version of the Dry Swings drill (see drill B3 on page 142). The rest of the team should sit on the bench in the actual batting order, with the first player after the on-deck batter at the end of the bench (at the start of the game, this would be the third batter in the lineup).

Your team should always sprint on and off the field and must always sit on the bench in the specified batting order. This will keep players from batting out of order and will remind them when it is time to jump into the on-deck circle and get ready to bat. It also keeps their attention on their teammates and the game.

Chatter

Whether on defense or offense, you should encourage your players to "talk it up" for their teammates. Continual encouragement and support from teammates boosts the confidence of the pitcher or the batter, and it keeps everyone's mind alert and focused on the game. Make it clear to your players that chatter does not include any derogatory words directed toward the other team, nor should it be advice or criticism. Tell them that you'll give advice and criticism if you think it's necessary, and that their job is to keep the bench and the defense alive with support. Particularly encourage players on the bench to offer support, and remember to tell them when they do a good job of helping their pitcher through a tough spot in the game, or for raising the level of intensity during a crucial at bat.

Playing with Heart

As 17-year-olds, we had made it to the Final Five of the American Legion State Tournament in Massachusetts. Our team was a ragtag bunch of skinny and not-so-skilled players who loved and expected to win ball games. We had won a number of dramatic come-from-behind contests just to make it to that point in the season, and in our first game of the tournament we had done it again. After tying the game in the ninth inning, we finally pushed across the winning run against a much more impressive and skilled club in the 12th inning. The stands were full of major league scouts, one of whom was from the Cincinnati Reds. He approached our coach after the game, shook his hand and said, "I've gotta admit—like the rest of us [scouts], I'm not really interested in any of your boys. But I wanted to shake your hand. If we could teach our players to play with the kind of heart that your boys showed tonight, we'd be contenders every year."

Players on the Bench

In addition to maintaining consistent chatter, players on the bench need other responsibilities that keep them involved in the game. By staying in the game mentally, they will be more ready to play when their turn comes. There are three important jobs that must be done by bench players: first-base coaching, retrieving foul balls, and keeping the equipment in order and out of the field of play. Encourage the bench players to organize a first-base coaching rotation in which a different player assumes the responsibility each inning during your time at bat. The first-base coach needs to always wear a helmet and is responsible for reminding any teammate who reaches first base about the number of outs. Bench players can also develop a rotation in which a different player each inning is responsible for retrieving the foul balls that leave the park. Although not a glamorous job, this is an important task, and you need to offer praise to the players who do it faithfully. These players also need to make sure that the bats, balls, helmets, and catcher's equipment are kept in order and out of the field of play. A foul ball that drifts over toward loose equipment strewn on the ground can be very dangerous. Finally, you can keep the players alert and having fun by periodically quizzing them on the number of outs, the count on the batter, and what they would do if the ball were hit to them. A healthy bench atmosphere is key to the character of the team, and a good mood is contingent upon the bench players feeling like an integral part of the action.

Third-Base Coaching

When your team is at bat, you become the third-base coach, who is responsible for giving signs or instructions to the batter and runners, reminding players of the number of outs, and instructing runners rounding second and third base. Signs can become very complicated, but at the youth level you need to keep signs clear and simple. Before each game, review your signs and game strategy with your team. Include signs for the bunt, the steal, and the take. If there is a runner on base, give a series of signs before each pitch. If you make touching your belt the sign for *bunt*, then the batter should bunt any time you use this sign. The same goes for giving the steal sign to a runner. The *take* sign refers to letting the next pitch go by regardless of whether it is a ball or a strike. Each of these plays, and the opportune times to attempt them, are explained below, along with how to guide base runners as they round the bases.

Most important, however, with regard to implementing offensive plays is the approach you bring to the third-base box. Calling plays is not a cut-and-dried science. Though there are better times to attempt a bunt or a hit-and-run than others, there are no set rules, and in fact, good game coaching often includes doing what is unexpected. There are times when great coaching decisions are foiled by poor execution, and other times when the wrong call produces a good result. So don't become overly anxious about these decisions; it's the fun that comes from execution and playing the game that are the most significant lessons learned in this area.

Key Elements
The Bunt

Most of the time when you give the bunt sign, you are asking the batter to *sacrifice bunt*, not to bunt-for-a-hit (see the fundamentals of bunting on pages 62–64). A sacrifice is always executed with a runner or runners on base and most commonly with players on first or second base. The term *sacrifice* comes from the fact that you are, in essence, sacrificing an out in order to advance the base runner(s). In executing a sacrifice, the batter squares and lays down the bunt allowing the runner or runners on first or second base to advance one base while the bunter is thrown out at first. But exactly *when* to attempt such a play is not so fundamental. Your decision depends on the batter and her particular strengths and on the game situation. At the youth level of play, often a well-placed sacrifice bunt will end up a hit or cause a throwing error. You may not be giving up an out.

If the batter is a player who struggles at the plate and perhaps is afraid of the ball, bunting can be a great way to get this player involved in the action, and can make him feel like a positive contributor to the team. Other times, however, though you may encounter a good bunting situation, the batter may be more confident swinging than bunting—so let her swing away. *Work on players' weaknesses in practice*—drill the struggling hitter with lots of swings and give the weak bunter extra bunts—*but try to coach toward players' strengths in games*. Though a good rule to follow, this won't always be the right move. There will be situations when to swing away or to bunt are the correct plays regardless of the batter.

The closer and lower the score, and the later it is in the game, the more prudent it becomes to sacrifice bunt. Remember, you are willing to *sacrifice* an out in order to advance a base runner, possibly two. If the game is close—tied or within one run—you may be willing to make this sacrifice

Baseball: A Game of Numbers

Baseball is a game of numbers. Every aspect of the game—fielding, pitching, batting, base running, you name it—can be recorded. These statistics can be helpful for you to use as a way of showing your players the areas in which they are strong as a team and the areas in which they need work. Always use stats to challenge and encourage your team, and never to discourage. For example, you may say in practice, "We had 12 hits and stole 4 bases last game—signs of a healthy and aggressive offense—but we had some defensive problems." Without saying that your team committed 14 errors, you can challenge them to focus on defensive work in practice and still keep the atmosphere positive. But on the other hand, it is important to discourage individual players from becoming concerned with their own personal stats. A group of players becomes a team when it disregards individual pursuits and glory. And a team has fun when it finds joy in collective accomplishment. Players focusing too much on personal statistics can destroy a good team-first attitude.

in order to move a runner into scoring position. This is particularly true if the game is low-scoring and in the later innings. If it is the fifth or sixth inning, that one run scored by bunting might prove to be the difference between winning and losing, but if it is still early in the game, sacrificing an out, and hence the possibility for a "big inning" of hitting and scoring, may cost your team several runs. Furthermore, a low-scoring game indicates that it has been difficult to score runs—perhaps the pitching has been particularly strong—and one run becomes all the more valuable. Thus, it is key that you continually evaluate the game situation and the ability of the batter at the plate.

Bunting at the youth level offers two other variables to consider. Because passed balls that skip behind the catcher are so common, it is often wise for runners to simply wait for this "free pass" in order to advance on the base paths. But, on the other hand, fielding a bunt and making the relatively difficult throw to first base is not as "automatic" at this level as it is with older players.

Being in "scoring position" refers to the position of base runners who are most likely to score on a base hit. A base hit is most likely to score a player from second base and will, most definitely, score even the slowest running player from third base. As a result, getting players to second base—by a hit, bunt, or steal—becomes an important task for the offense. A team with a runner on second is just one hit away from scoring a run.

Though not as common a play, bunting for a hit is an important play to consider. Players on your team who have displayed the ability to bunt for a hit should be given the green light to do so whenever they are at bat with no one on base, unless the defense takes the bunt away. With no one on, you can also give players the bunt sign, which implies that you intend for them to bunt for a hit. If the opposing third baseman is positioned exceptionally deep, it might be an appropriate time to attempt to drop a bunt down the third-base line.

The Steal

Stealing is not as significant a part of the game at the youth level as it is when players get older for two major reasons. First, base runners are not allowed to leave the base until the ball crosses home plate, making a successful steal quite difficult. And second, because of the large number of passed balls that skip past catchers, which result in all but a free pass to the next base for runners, it often doesn't pay to take the chance of stealing. However, if the catcher seems particularly reliable, and you need that runner on first base to be on second so that she is in scoring position, giving the sign to steal can be the good call.

If so, the rules and technique are simple. Base runners, whether preparing to steal or not, should always begin with their rear foot on the base, and the lead foot already extended toward the next base. This should appear something like a sprinter's starting position. As soon as the pitch crosses home plate, the runner can take off. He sprints without looking at the infielder covering the base and slides in a direction away from the throw. This is not a force play, thus the fielder must tag the runner for the runner to be called out.

The Take

When you give a batter the *take* sign, you are instructing her not to swing at the next pitch. You might give this sign in a couple of situations. If the opposing pitcher is having real control problems, and you are in need of base runners, have the batter take the first pitch. The chance of that first pitch being a ball is high, and hitting when one is "ahead in the count" (there are more balls than strikes) is much easier than when one is behind. By giving the take sign, you are avoiding the chance of your batter swinging at a pitch that is out of the strike zone and, in effect, putting herself in an unnecessary hole. Plus, you are increasing the chance of being issued a base on balls. You may also want to give the take sign when your first two batters in an inning hit the first or second pitches for outs. If this happens, you already have two outs against you, and you haven't made the pitcher

Baseball: A Humbling but Great Game

Good players play the game hard and have great respect for the game, their coaches, and teammates. Young players need to understand how difficult it is to play and learn the game—and to realize that it takes a lifetime of practice to hone their skills. No matter how good you think you are, at each level, on a given day, the game can humble you. Learn from past mistakes, but think about the next pitch, the next at bat, the next opportunity. Have a team-first attitude. Do what you can to help the team win. Take pride in your team, your teammates, and your own play. Baseball can be a frustrating game, but the game can also give you great pleasure and satisfaction. Very few athletes can play the game successfully. There will be adjustments, and new challenges at each level. Take a lot of personal pride in what you've learned and accomplished and look forward to the next challenge.

work. If the third batter should hit the first pitch for an out, your defense will be back on the field with virtually no rest or chance to regroup. By giving the take sign to this third batter in the inning, you are trying to at least make the pitcher throw a few more pitches, give your team a bit more time on offense, and avoid putting your defense immediately back onto the field.

But aside from a few circumstances in which the take is appropriate, *let your players hit*. Instructing them to take too many pitches runs contrary to trying to instill an aggressive mental approach to batting. Really encourage players at this age to be aggressive hitters and not fear making an out. Their goal is to hit the ball hard.

Instructing the Base Runners

As the third-base coach, you are also responsible for giving instructions to the base runners as they are running the bases. Specifically, you are responsible for runners on second and third, while it is the first-base coach's responsibility to handle runners at first. Because you have a better vantage point of surveying the field than the runners, you can help them make wise base-running decisions. The instructions you give include signaling them to round a base and continue on to the next one, to stay at a base, or to slide. If you want a runner to continue to the next base, signal it by circling your left arm like a windmill. If you want him to stay at a base but not to slide, hold both of your arms and hands up and call, "Hold the bag!" And if you want a player to slide, energetically wave and point your arms toward the ground and call, "Down! Down!" Remember: be conservative on defense, but be aggressive on offense. This includes running the bases. Throwing someone out from the outfield is a very difficult task because it requires a good throw, catch, and tag. Force the opposing team to make such a play, and if they do, applaud them for it. That's good baseball.

When to Visit the Mound

If your pitcher is throwing well, let her go. Don't interrupt her rhythm or concentration—just keep encouraging her from the bench. But if she begins to struggle with control or concentration, you may want to consider paying her a visit.

You are allowed to visit the pitcher on the mound once per inning without replacing him as pitcher, but if you visit a second time in one inning, you must replace him with another pitcher. He can stay in the game, but he cannot continue to pitch.

Though there is no rule for when you should visit your pitcher on the mound, there are certainly signs that indicate that a visit might be a good idea. If your pitcher issues three walks in a row, it would be wise to go out and ask if anything is wrong—perhaps soreness or fatigue. Also, if a pitcher becomes terribly frustrated because she can't seem to get anyone out, or she can't seem to throw consistent strikes, try to get her refocused. And if you notice a specific problem with her mechanics that you think she might be willing and able to fix during the game, go out and give her instruction. But if you are not going with the intent of making a pitching change, or to make a specific suggestion regarding her mechanics, or to find out if your pitcher is injured, offer encouragement. If she is frustrated, smile and reassure her that she will be fine, that you and the team are behind her, and that she can get the next batter out. You need to get to know your pitchers well enough to determine which ones pitch through adversity better than others. For some pitchers, to be left out on the mound to fight through a tough inning is torture, and you would be better off making a change. But for others, though they are frustrated, they want to get through it themselves and come back strong the next inning. Take pride in knowing your kids and pushing them to their respective limits, but at the same time respect those limits.

When Nothing Seems to Be Going Right

One of the great mysteries of baseball is its unexplainable contagious nature! On some days it seems as if your team couldn't make an error if they were trying to and that every batter—from 1 through 9—is smacking hits. But, unfortunately, on other days it seems as if your defense isn't using gloves, and your bats all have holes. When the good days come along, just hold your breath and enjoy them. But when the bad days rear up, that's when you earn your millions as a coach. After a particularly difficult inning in the field, bring the whole team together in a huddle, downplay the errors, tell them to forget about that inning, and challenge them to take out their frustration with the bats. If your team can't seem to hit, encourage them to be more aggressive—to swing at first pitches. If they are swinging at poor pitches and frequently striking out, have them take the first pitch and encourage them to be more selective. Always be encouraging, and work hard to stifle negative comments from players and from your own mouth. Be particularly concerned with teammates who become angry with one another or speak in hostile tones. Take them aside and let them know that win, lose, or draw, you are a team and must treat one another with respect. Most of all, retain a sense of humor, and without downplaying the significance of working hard to execute techniques properly, keep the atmosphere positive.

Taking Stock after the Game

After each game is a good time to assess where you are and where you want to be. It can be tempting to focus entirely on the number of runs scored and to concentrate solely on the your win-loss record as indicators of how the team is doing. If you are winning games, the season is going great; if you're losing, the season is going poorly. Rather than allowing game scores and team records to dictate the status of your season, remember that the whole point of coaching your players is to help them become better base-ball players, individually and as a team, and learning how to compete.

Games have a wonderful way of revealing a team's strengths and exposing its weaknesses. Use games as vehicles for evaluating progress in skill development and in how well your players are coming together as a team. The first question you should ask yourself is, Are the players improving individually? Make a checklist of the different skill areas, check through the growth book, and assess how each player is developing and progressing in these skills. The skill areas include

- Catching fly balls and throws
- Throwing accuracy
- Fielding ground balls
- Throwing strikes
- Batting aggressively, making contact
- Hustling regardless of the situation
- Keeping chatter consistent and positive
- Playing with energy, focus, and enthusiasm

Take note of each player's development of these skills in the growth book and in practice encourage individual players to focus on areas of weakness. Then look at the team as a whole and try to assess their overall performance on defense, batting, pitching, and attitude. Congratulate your players on the aspects of the game that they do well. When you can pinpoint problems your team has during games, take the problem apart piece by piece and see how you can address it. Most often the problem will be something that needs to be addressed in practice.

Here are several common problems that young teams have and some ways to address them.

Problem: We're Making Too Many Infield Errors

Errors are double-edged swords: they force a defense to make extra plays, and they allow runners on base that otherwise wouldn't be there. On top of that, they frustrate pitchers and can embarrass and humble young players.

It's important to first determine how these errors are committed. Is it from a lack of skill, fear of the ball, or that a player is playing out of position?

Solution

Attack the baseball

If the problem is with botching ground balls, most likely players are letting the ball play them—they are not aggressively approaching the ball. During the All at Shortstop drill (see drill D5 on pages 126–27) and throughout infield practice, encourage your infielders to keep their approach toward the ball and their weight on the balls of their feet as they glide into their stance.

This brings the hands down to the ground and out in front of the body, and it allows fielders to adjust to various hops.

Practice with pressure

You may notice that your infielders make accurate throws in practice, but not in games. If errant throws are the problem, the solution is to practice with pressure. The added pressure of a base runner sprinting toward first base often causes poor infield throws. In practice, add an extra session of the Ground Balls at Positions drill (see drill D12 on pages 130–31) and add base runners into the mix. Over and over, hit ground balls to your infielders and let them get used to the added pressure and the amount of time that they actually have to make the play. Having players running to first base even off fungoed ground balls is a great learning experience for infielders, it's challenging, and it's game-like.

Problem: We Don't Score Enough Runs

Your players are working hard in practice on the hitting drills and are making good contact during the Live Hitting drill (see drill B6 on page 143), but they're having trouble putting runs up on the board.

Solution

Swing the bat

If your team has been hitting well in practice but can't seem to get it going in games, encourage your batters to go after the first good pitch to hit. Many hitters let this pitch go by because they're nervous and they figure that there are still at least two more chances to swing. The problem is, the first pitch is often the best pitch to hit. Go after it. Encourage them to adjust their mental approach and to think: "I'm going to jump all over the first good pitch."

Be more selective

The first solution might be completely wrong, however. Check the statistics and find out if you're drawing many walks. If not, maybe your team is swinging too liberally. Perhaps players are striking out on pitches out of the strike zone or are making poor contact with tough pitches. During the Live Hitting drill (see drill B6 on page 143), give your players actual counts and encourage them to swing at strikes but to let balls go by. Train their "batting eyes" to be selective of good pitches and to take the tough pitches.

Run the bases aggressively

Perhaps your players are getting on base, but they aren't making it home. Work hard, as the third-base coach, to get players into scoring positions and then be aggressive in sending them home on base hits or other plays. Many coaches quote the unwritten rule that you never should make the first or third out at third base, because a player can also score from second base on a base hit and thus to chance an out at third is not worth it. At the youth level there are many ways to score from third base that don't work from second. A passed ball, an error, a fielder's choice, a dropped fly ball—all of these situations result in a run if you already have a base runner on third base. But if the runner is on second base, he will remain stranded on the base paths until something else happens that brings him in. At this level, aggressiveness usually pays big dividends.

Problem: We Make a Lot of Mental Errors

The pressure of a game situation and the fact that baseball is a complicated game can often result in players making mental errors. A common mental error is throwing to the wrong base or making an unnecessary throw.

Solution

Listen to the field generals

The field generals, often the catcher, shortstop, or center fielder, keep the defense alert and aware of the game situation. Before each new batter, and sometimes before each pitch, these selected players call out the number of outs and let their teammates know what they should do with the ball if it is hit at them. Drills such as Situations Off Fungo Hits (see drill E1 on page 146), Soft-Toss Scrimmage (see drill E2 on page 146), and even Infield Practice (drill D25 on pages 139–40) provide good opportunities for field generals to practice their verbal responsibilities to the team. These drills also help the rest of the team grow accustomed to hearing their calls and anticipating the proper reaction to a batted ball.

CHAPTER 8

Dealing with Parents and Gender Issues

Perspective on Parents

Coaches have to realize that it's nearly impossible for parents to properly evaluate their own child's ability. I know this firsthand—I'm a parent, and I've seen my own daughter rise up through youth league sports. I've also seen it throughout my 35 years of coaching. We all love our kids; we talk about them in glowing terms, and we wish that everything would go right for them, regardless of the activity. If it's youth-league basketball, you want every shot to go in and every rebound to be theirs. If they're playing Little League baseball, you wish they would get a hit every time, and you hate to see them make an error. You want them to do well so they'll feel as good about themselves as you do. The problem is that parents just can't be as realistic about their children's abilities as a coach can. And as a coach, you need to understand and appreciate that. Situations are bound to arise where you will have to address a parent's expectations versus the reality of the situation, but the key is to communicate, and in a very honest but tactful manner.

The main thing in dealing with parents, without question, is to keep the lines of communication open. Don't detour from your philosophy as a coach and what you want out of your players. Keep all the principles in mind when you're dealing with parents. There may be times when you disagree and when you'll have to tell the parents that you disagree with what they are saying. Explain that you are running the program the best way you can, and hope that they'll understand your viewpoint.

It's also good to have some kind of ongoing communication with parents. Regular letters sent home throughout the season can cover logistics, schedule changes, reminders of needs and a review of the season thus far. You can use these communications to offer an upbeat tone about the team and their children's efforts, no matter how well the team is doing in the win-loss column. Some kind of fun picnic or potluck dinner at midseason is also a great way to maintain communication, enabling you to have contact with the parents other than just when they are unhappy about something.

Be Organized at All Times

Many potential misunderstandings between coaches and parents are caused by a lack of organization on the coaches' part. Perhaps the coaches haven't been clear about their expectations for the season or about their philosophy of coaching, playing, and substitution. You'll need to make sure that you are well organized and are communicating your expectations clearly and openly through the letter you send at the beginning of the season and the atmosphere you create with the players. Parents appreciate this honesty and fairness.

Help Parents Look at the Big Picture

Parents need to realize that there are many players on your team, and that your interest and concern is for all of them, not for one or two. You may occasionally have parents whose expectation levels are so high that if their children aren't excelling on the field immediately after joining the team, there is something wrong with the coach and the program. You may need to remind parents that everyone has a beginning step; encourage them to judge the progress not so much on productivity or success during the game but by how much the players are enjoying the game and learning new skills. Gently remind parents that the success of their children is measured by the improvement in their skills and their continued high interest and love for the game and competition.

Addressing Gender Issues

When it comes to dealing with young kids, the fewer rules in regard to gender issues, the better. Kids in particular have a real way of sorting things out. If I have a coed team and say to a group of players, "Okay, let's pair up and play catch," it's very likely that the top two players will be paired up, and if we have a couple of weaker players, there's a good chance they will be paired up. In the same way, if we have two girls, they will most likely pair up to do the drill. That just happens—kids don't necessarily take gender into account when they are choosing partners for drills, they choose the person most like them in ability. Try to let your players sort themselves out, regardless of gender—you will probably find that players of like ability will pair up.

Often, if you just let things happen and don't create an issue out of something that isn't one to your players, everybody becomes more comfortable with whatever situation works out. But at the same time, if you have one or two girls on your team, you need to make a conscious effort to integrate them into the team. Use them to demonstrate certain drills, or single out their technique or work ethic as an example after which players should be striving. There is a balance to strike between not making an issue out of a non-issue and providing support and attention to the girls on your team, who may feel, at least at first, somewhat uncomfortable. With the younger kids, try and encourage a variety of different groupings. Whether people are right-handed or lefthanded, whatever their race or gender, the principles of being a team—playing together, respecting their effort, not criticizing each other, and supporting one another—should be paramount.

A baseball player needs to learn a variety of different skills, and each skill requires the use of a variety of different muscles. I have discussed throughout the book the difficulty that many young players have with certain skills due to immature muscular development. Girls often develop earlier than boys until the age of 12 or 13, and as a result, they are often as capable or more capable of performing many of these skills. For this reason, I would certainly teach the same techniques to both girls and boys. But it is also true that the physiology and development of girls is different from boys. Because of the significant difference specifically in shoulder development as they grow through the teenage years, I would steer girls away from pitching. The stress and strain on the shoulder may be too great, and the overhand throwing technique may increase the potential for injury as girls begin to throw with more velocity.

Girls also tend to take criticism very personally, and they also are more apt to want to know the rationale behind a particular drill or skill, whereas many boys will run through a wall if the coach tells them to, and they wouldn't question why they were doing it. You won't have to change any drills or your coaching philosophy if you're coaching girls. Just be prepared to offer them more information and probably a bit more direction. You'll find that the girls are every bit as competitive as boys and often much more coachable. It's all in how you bring that competitive spirit out of them.

That being said, whereas younger kids often compete against each other across gender up to the sixth or seventh grade, by then teams should be single gender if possible. Otherwise, boys tend to dominate the play, and the differences in the learning styles for girls and boys, as well as their emotional differences, make it a good idea to have separate teams. Girls and boys are motivated in different ways, so what works with the girls may fail miserably with the boys. Athletics is a natural place for girls to develop confidence and assertive behavior, and by junior high the presence of boys can diminish the experience—maybe not for all girls or in every situation, but certainly for some. By this age, sports should be separate from the boy-girl stuff that will certainly be starting for many kids, making them self-conscious with the opposite gender.

Questions and Answers about Dealing with Parents

Q. I have some parents who keep giving their kids "advice" about their performance after games and practices, but I really disagree with their suggestions. How do I address this?

A. The temptation might be to single out the parents after practice and let them know who's running the ship, but that is not the answer. Parents will be and need to be involved in teaching and raising their children, and you are a small part of the equation. What is important to observe is how the youngster is responding to your coaching. Is he confused by the opposing ideas that he's hearing regarding certain skills, or does he seem to follow your lead during practice? If his parents' advice seems to be affecting his performance and attitude, you'll want to address that specific issue with them. But don't discuss different philosophies of instruction with a parent unless the parent raises the question.

Q. Some parents insist on sitting right behind the bench and make comments during the game about the other team and the umpiring. I know they are trying to be supportive to the kids and the team, but I don't like it. What's a diplomatic solution here?

A. This is where the preseason letter becomes so important. Be clear in that note about the expectations for coaches, players, *and* parents regarding good sportsmanship. Explain that baseball is a chance to teach kids the skills of the game and, more important, valuable lessons on respect, discipline, and positive behavior. Then, if the situation with a parent becomes out-of-hand, you can discreetly point out to the parent the importance of modeling sportsmanship to the kids.

Q. Some of my players feel very bad that their parents aren't at all interested in what they are doing. How can I encourage these parents to be more supportive and to participate more in their kids' activities?

A. The preseason letter and phone call are done, in part, to solicit parental help in a variety of areas. Feel free to call these parents again and to determine their level of availability and willingness to help. If you express need with regard to a specific task, often parents will be willing to pitch in. Whether it is a setting up a bake sale, organizing rides, or hitting fungoes, all parents have something they can give if they have the time and interest.

Q. I have a parent who constantly questions my judgment about how much time each team member plays. She feels that her child, who is quite good, is not playing enough. I have explained that it is important for every team member to play, regardless of ability. We simply don't see eye-to-eye on this, and the parent cannot accept my explanation.

A. At the first meeting of the season with both parents and players, ask the kids whether they would rather play and lose a game or sit on the bench and win. Inevitably, the kids will opt to play the game, and the parents, standing behind the kids, are witnesses to the fact that the players themselves want equal playing time. Let it be known at that point, to both the parents and kids, that you will schedule equal playing time for each team member, regardless of the game situation. No parent, then, can argue during the season that his or her child should be playing more than any other. You and the kids themselves endorse the equal playing time rule, a rule to which you will remain consistent.

Q. I have a parent who is incredibly critical of his child. He has a negative way of shouting orders to his child when she's playing and then instructs her when she's on the bench about how she should have done something differently. How can I diplomatically ask the parent to back off and adopt a more positive attitude?

A. It is very important that you explain to the parent what you are trying to do as a coach—namely that you are teaching proper fundamentals and creating a positive and learner-friendly environment in which players feel comfortable taking chances and are not afraid of failure. Tell him that it is confusing and counterproductive if too many people are coaching during time on the field. Most often the parent will come to recognize and respect your approach.

    With this problem, as well as with other difficult situations involving parents, make sure that you address the problem immediately. Don't avoid speaking up. Send a letter home after a few games reminding the parent of your expectations and goals. If the behavior persists, approach the parent directly.

Questions and Answers about Gender Issues

Q. I have a team of both boys and girls. In the drills the girls always tend to pair up with girls and the boys pair up with boys rather than matching up by equal skill level. Should I let them do this, or should I pair them by skill level regardless of gender?

A. If they are choosing their own partners and seem happy with their partner relationships, let it be. In other words, if no issue develops, don't make one. But when you are assigning groups, positions, or partners, mix the boys and girls. Show your team that you recognize no preference or difference with respect to players' abilities.

Q. My team has only one girl on it. She seems very comfortable and confident with the boys, but some of the boys are not comfortable with her. What should I do?

A. This represents a great opportunity to address and reinforce the principle that each player on the team is equal in importance and fills an important role on the team. Use the entire season as the time frame to teach this lesson. Stress during every practice and game the importance of valuing each individual on the team. Find something that this girl does well and praise her for it. Even young players will recognize and respect good effort, hustle, and performance. Point out the ways that she works and contributes and is important to the team, and watch how the boys' attitudes are transformed.

PART TWO

Drills: The Foundation for Development, Success, Happiness, and a Coach's Peace of Mind

CHAPTER 9

Warm-Up: Base Running, Catching, and Throwing

Arm Swings W1

Purpose: To practice proper arm motion for sprinting.

Have your players stand along an outfield foul line with their arms at right angles and close to their bodies. They should swing their arms as if they were running, using a "chest to the hip pocket" length of swing with their hands. Encourage them to maintain right angles with their elbows as they swing.

Running in Place W2

Purpose: To work on proper sprinting form.

In this drill, players stand in place and rise as high on the balls of their feet as possible. Their heels should be off the ground. Have them run in place, continuing to land high on the balls of their feet, leaning forward from the heels. Remind them to use proper arm swings.

Jog-Sprint W3

Purpose: To practice proper sprinting form by starting in a jog and ending in a full sprint.

Place one cone or field marker five yards out and then another cone ten yards beyond the first. Line up your players along the first-base foul line. At your signal, players will jog out into the field, concentrating on lifting their knees high, landing on the balls of the feet, and reaching out with their lower legs. When they reach the first marker, they sprint until they reach the second marker, where they will turn around and jog easily back to their original starting point, again concentrating on lifting knees high and landing on the balls of their feet. Repeat the exercise three to five times, each time increasing in speed.

Note that in all of the following drills, players should work on proper running form as indicated above.

Home to First Base W4

Purpose: To practice sprinting through first base, simulating what a runner does after hitting a ground ball to an infielder.

This drill helps players beat the throw from an infielder by staying out of the way of the incoming ball. Line up your players at home plate, one after another. On your signal, at two-second intervals, each player imitates a swing and sprints through first base, veering off into foul territory after reaching the base. They then jog back to home plate in foul territory and away from the first-base line.

Home to Second Base W5

Purpose: To practice rounding first base and sprinting to second base, simulating hitting a double.

In this drill players run from home to second base, working on rounding the inside corner of first base. Place an object (a cone, shoe, hat, or some other object) 8–10 feet before first base approximately and 3–4 feet into foul territory. Line up your players at home plate, one after another. On your signal, at two-second intervals, each player imitates a swing and runs with the intention of legging out a double. The players should approach first base with a slight arc (a circle turn) and run to the right of the object. As they approach the base, they should look at and tag the *inside* of the base and push off toward second base in as straight a line as possible. Make sure each player gets out of the way quickly after touching second base.

First Base to Third Base W6

Purpose: To practice rounding second base on the way to third, simulating a base runner advancing on a teammate's base hit to the outfield.

This drill helps players running the bases to learn to always watch for the directives of the third base coach. In this drill, either you or an assistant is at third base. Line up your players at first base. At your signal, each player sprints toward second base, simulating the advance made on a base hit. As

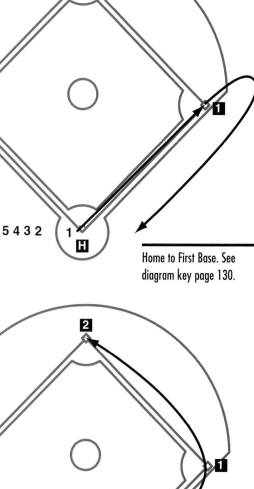

Home to First Base. See diagram key page 130.

Home to Second Base

First Base to Third Base

Second Base to Home

each player approaches second base, he should look to third for the third base coach who, in a game, would tell the player whether to stay at second or to keep running to third base. The player should then look back down toward second base and perform the proper rounding technique. As he rounds second base he should again look to the third base coach, who will tell him to either stop at third standing up, slide into third, or go home.

Second Base to Home W7

Purpose: To practice rounding third base on the way to home plate, simulating a base runner scoring on a base hit to the outfield.

This drill, like First Base to Third Base (see drill W6), helps your player focus on the visual instructions of the third-base coach. In this drill, you or your assistant is at third base. Line up your players on second base. At your signal they will sprint, one at a time, from second base to third to home plate. As players set up to round third, the third-base coach tells them either to stay at third base or sprint for home. This is a fast drill, so make sure your players run through the base (or home plate) and get out of the way of the next runner.

Tagging Up W8

Purpose: To practice tagging up from third base on a fly ball to the outfield.

Have your players line up at third base. In turn, each player starts with one foot on the base and listens to your description of the hit: "Fly ball to right. Tag up!" She should look toward right field, and when you say, "Go!" (which means that the ball was caught), she should sprint through home plate. Vary the location of the imaginary fly ball with each runner.

Five-in-One Drill W9

Purpose: To practice five different base-running situations at one time.

Place three runners at the five base running positions shown in the diagram on the next page. At your signal, each runner sprints his assigned distance. There are five different running distances:

- Runner A: Runs home to first base.
- Runner B: Runs home to second base, using the circle turn technique.
- Runner C: Runs first base to third base.
- Runner D: Runs second base to home.
- Runner E: Tags up from third base on a fly ball.

All five runners sprint at the same time. When they reach their respective bases, signal the next five players to go. Remind your players to work on proper running form, rounding the bases, tagging the bases, and pushing off the bags. Extra runners or players who have just performed the drill stand near their base and always to the side of the diamond. (intermediate)

Tagging Up

Bent-Leg Slide W10

Purpose: To work on the proper sliding technique for youth players. This drill should be taught as a progression.

Have your players practice the proper sliding technique: sitting down, stationary, with the top leg out, reaching for the base, and the bottom leg tucked up and underneath the thigh of the top leg. The player's back should lay back when sliding so too much weight is not forward.

Once your players have a good handle on the proper sliding technique from a stationary position, have them practice it on the field at half speed. Have as many players executing the drill at one time as you have bases. At first, it is best to practice on soft and/or wet grass. Using a detached base, each player starts the slide 6 to 7 feet before the base.

The following are the steps each player takes in executing a bent-leg slide.

Five-in-One Drill

1. Takeoff from the underneath (bent) leg. The takeoff leg always becomes the bent leg.
2. Keep body weight low to the ground. The body should glide in to the base, not jump.
3. Keep the body and legs relaxed.

4. The bent leg should be flexed up to 90 degrees at the knee, and the ankle and instep should be curled upward so as not to catch the cleats in the ground.
5. Weight should be distributed on the calf, thigh, and buttocks of the bent leg. The outer calf hits the ground first and takes most of the landing force.
6. The top leg should be flexed and relaxed in order to absorb the force of contacting the base.
7. Tag the base with the heel and instep of the top foot.

As your players improve in doing a bent-leg slide, have them extend the slide in the following ways:

- Sliding at half-speed from a 30-foot distance
- Sliding at full speed from a 30-foot distance
- Sliding at full speed in various base-running drills, such as Home to Second Base (see drill W5) and First Base to Third Base (see drill W6)

Catching the Ball

The following drills are meant to be taught as a progression.

Above, below, and at Waist High   W11

Purpose: To establish the fundamentals of catching without the added fear of being struck by the ball. This progression includes proper footwork, glove positioning, using two hands, and organizing the feet.

This drill should be done without a ball. Stand facing the outfield between the pitcher's mound and home plate while your players are positioned throughout the infield facing you. As you call out the command, "Ready . . . catch!" they respond by simulating a catch with the following techniques. Players perform two or three repetitions for each stage.

- Ball above the waist.
    1. Players step toward the ball with the glove-side foot.
    2. Players' fingers are positioned above the ball. They catch the top of the ball using two hands.
    3. Players grab a seam on the baseball and simultaneously organize their feet into the proper throwing position. They practice quick feet and proper throwing arm action up to the cocked position.

- Ball below the waist.
    1. Players step toward the ball with the glove-side foot.
    2. Players' fingers are positioned below the ball. They catch the middle-bottom of the ball using two hands.
    3. Players grab a seam on the baseball and simultaneously organize their feet into the proper throwing position. They practice quick feet and proper throwing arm action to the cocked position.

- Ball at the waist.
    1. Players step toward the ball with the glove-side foot. They flex their knees in order to drop the waist below the ball.
    2. Players' fingers are positioned above the ball. They catch the top of the ball using two hands.
    3. Players grab a seam on the baseball and simultaneously organize their feet into the proper throwing position. They practice quick feet and proper throwing arm action to the cocked position.

After you have completed this entire progression without players using a ball, repeat the drill using Incredi-balls (or, if you don't have them, substitute tennis balls). Have your players choose partners and make under-hand tosses to each other from 15–20 feet away. The player catching the ball needs to practice the same fundamentals learned in the drill using no ball. Finally, when players are comfortable catching the Incredi-balls, switch to using baseballs. Your team will pick up the drill quickly, and the progression will speed up each time you do it. After spending time on this drill progression, players will be prepared to perform a normal catch-and-throw warm-up using proper catching and throwing techniques.

Ball to Glove-Side Drill W12

Purpose: To learn the proper footwork related to catching a throw or a fly ball that comes to the glove side of the body. This drill follows the same progression explained in Above, below, and at the Waist (see drill W11).

In this progression, instead of stepping directly toward the ball, each player steps at a 45-degree angle toward the ball with the glove-side foot (left foot for right-handed throwers and right foot for lefties). Because of this step, each player needs to sweep the throwing-side foot behind the other leg in order to properly organize the feet for throwing. Use proper throwing arm action.

Ball to Throwing-Side Drill W13

Purpose: To learn the proper footwork related to catching a throw or a fly ball that comes to the throwing-hand side of the body. This drill follows the same progression explained in Above, below, and at the Waist (see drill W11).

In this progression, each player steps at a 45-degree angle toward the ball with the throwing-side foot. Because of this footwork, the feet are already in position for throwing, and the player needs only to step with the lead foot and throw.

Backhand Drill W14

Purpose: To learn the proper footwork related to catching a throw or a fly ball that comes to the far backhand of the body (that is, to the far throwing-hand side of the body). This drill follows the same progression explained in Above, below, and at the Waist (see drill W11).

In this progression, a right-handed thrower crosses his left foot over his right and catches the ball with just the glove-hand, with his thumb pointing downward. After the catch, the right foot follows the left in order to organize the feet; he plants and throws. A left-handed thrower would use the opposite footwork.

Throw-and-Catch

Five Every Five W15

Purpose: To practice proper throwing and catching fundamentals while loosening up throwing arms. These fundamentals include proper footwork in catching, using two hands, organizing the feet to throw, proper arm action, and following-through. This drill is also designed to teach proper throwing techniques.

Divide your players into partners based on comparable arm strength. Have the partners stand across from each other approximately 30 to 40 feet apart. Using proper throwing and catching fundamentals learned in the progression drills, partners should throw and catch the ball back and forth, increasing their distance by 5 feet after every five throws. To do so, the player in the outfield takes two large steps backward. Partners should not go beyond a comfortable distance but should work on increasing the distance between them each practice.

Focus Drill W16

Purpose: To help players focus on practicing throwing accuracy.

This drill works well in conjunction with the Five Every Five drill (see drill W15). As your players are throwing and catching and moving back 5 steps every five catches, you call, "Focus Drill!" The partner preparing to catch the ball holds up her glove in random spots, and the thrower focuses on hitting the glove with each throw. Remind your players to make firm throws, using proper mechanics (foot planted perpendicular to the target, full arm extension, good follow-through) and to avoid "aiming" the ball (shortens arm action and arm extension during release of the ball, short-arms the follow-through causing a loss of velocity and control).

Quick Hand Drill W17

Purpose: To work on catching the ball with two hands, organizing the feet to throw, and to get rid of the ball as quickly and as accurately as possible. (easy–intermediate)

In this drill partners should be 30 feet apart, in good athletic position. At your signal, players throw and catch back and forth using proper technique, using two hands, and establishing quick, fluid rhythm. They should not throw especially hard but should practice quick hands and quick feet while working on ball exchange from the glove to the throwing hand (ball exchange). Also, the players should keep their feet moving. Perform this drill in 30-second bursts.

CHAPTER 10

Defensive Fundamentals: Infield Play, Outfield Play, and Team Defense

Infield

Ground Ball Work D1

Purpose: To practice the proper fundamentals of fielding ground balls including preparation, stance, and use of the hands. This series of drills also works on leg strength and general quickness. (easy–intermediate)

Each set of drills simulating different types of ground balls (Direct Ground Balls, see drill D2; Side-to-Side Ground Balls, see drill D3; and Forehands and Backhands, see drill D4) is performed in three stages:

1. Using bare hands
2. Using just the glove with the throwing-hand behind the back
3. Using both hands with the glove

Only in the third stage do the players need to practice organizing their feet for the throw, but in each stage of the drills they should practice the proper fundamentals of preparation, stance, and hands.

Pick-ups are done in pairs with one partner rolling 12 to 15 *easy* ground balls from 10 to 15 feet away to the fielder, who simply tosses the ball back to the roller. After each set of 12 to 15 grounders, the partners switch. Remind your fielders to maintain the proper stance throughout the drill in order to work on leg strength and good habits. The drill should not be rushed but should take only a minute or two for each round of ground balls.

Direct Ground Balls D2

Purpose: To practice proper fundamentals of fielding a ground ball, including preparation, stance, and use of the hands. Direct ground balls allows players to focus on the basics.

Refer to the Ground Ball Work drill (see drill D1) for a complete explanation of how to conduct this progression drill.

In this drill one partner rolls ground balls directly to the middle of the fielder's stance. The fielder should not come out of her stance to make the flip back to her partner but should remain down in a fielder's position throughout the drill.

Ground Ball Work: Side-to-Side Ground Balls D3

Purpose: To practice proper fundamentals of fielding a ground ball, including preparation, stance, and use of the hands while moving, or sliding, from side to side. This movement involves working on "rounding off" the ground ball.

Refer to the Ground Ball Work drill (see drill D1) for a complete explanation of how to conduct this progression drill.

In this drill one partner rolls 8 to 10 ground balls to the right, and then 8 to 10 to the left of the fielding partner, forcing him to shuffle his feet like a basketball defenseman in order to get his body in front of the ball. Ground balls should be rolled slowly enough to allow the fielder to *round off* on the ball. This means that not only does he move laterally, but he also takes a forward angle to the ball, which positions his body and feet in front of the ball.

Forehands and Backhands D4

Purpose: To practice proper fundamentals of fielding ground balls hit to the far glove-hand (forehand) and throwing-hand (backhand) side of the fielder. This includes working on proper footwork and glove positioning. (easy–intermediate)

Refer to the Ground Ball Work drill (see drill D1) for a complete explanation of how to conduct this progression drill.

In this drill one partner rolls 8 to 10 ground balls to the far right, then 8 to 10 to the left of the fielder, forcing her to move her feet and to field the ball outside of her body. Forehands, ground balls to the far glove-hand side, are fielded with the glove-side foot reaching toward the ball, and with the fingers on the ground and thumb up. Backhands, ground balls to the far throwing-hand side, are fielded with the glove-side foot crossing over the other foot, and with the glove low and the thumb down. Encourage your players to immediately move back into proper fielding position after fielding the ground balls.

All at Shortstop D5

Purpose: To work on fielding batted ground balls and to reinforce the same fundamentals learned doing ground ball technique work (see drill D1).

This drill is a very efficient way to help your infielders practice fielding ground balls. Have all your infield players line up one behind the other at shortstop. Every player takes a turn at shortstop, while you hit ground balls to them, short 50-foot fungoes or from home plate. Try to simulate the different types of ground balls previously practiced, and feel free to move closer to the players in order to improve your hitting accuracy. Give your players two ground balls apiece and encourage them to focus and work on something specific each time, such as being aggressive on the approach, or proper glove position. Incorporate one or two rounds of ground balls that force the players to range far to the right and left, and encourage them to dive for the ball. This is exactly what infielders want to do, and the kids will love it. Anywhere from 5 to 10 rounds of ground balls is appropriate, depending on your players' development. It is best to use Incredi-balls for this drill until your players have developed confidence and improved skills. One of your catchers can act as a shagger for the incoming throws back to you.

Field and Throw   D6

Purpose: To add the elements of organizing the feet by using the infield "toe-to-heel hop" and throwing to first base to the previous drills for fielding batted ground balls. (easy–intermediate)

This drill is similar to All at Shortstop (see drill D5), but this time players throw to first base after they've fielded the ground ball. One of the most important components of this drill is the *toe-to-heel, infielders crow-hop*: after a player fields the ground ball and as he comes up out of his fielding stance, he pushes off his rear foot and shuffles it toward his front foot. The toe of his rear foot nearly kicks the heel of his front foot, and then the player plants his rear foot perpendicular to the throwing target, steps, and throws to first base. Use a back-up first baseman in this drill to field errant throws.

Knockout   D7

Purpose: To create a fun and competitive environment of fielding ground balls. This game rewards proper fundamentals and aggressive infield play. (easy–intermediate)

Have all of your infielders line up at shortstop. In succession, each infielder fields one ground ball. If a player fields the ground ball cleanly or makes a good effort at keeping the ball in front of her after moving forward on the grounder, she goes to the end of the line and stays in the game. But if an error is made, or the player purposefully gets out of the way of the ground ball, she is "out" of the game. The last remaining fielder who has not committed an error must field one last ground ball cleanly—if she does, she wins; if she does not, the fungo hitter is declared the winner.

Hot Potato   D8

Purpose: To work on proper infield catching and throwing fundamentals and to perform these skills as quickly as possible. This game rewards quickness and "sure hands." (intermediate)

Divide your players into groups of four. Players will throw and catch to each other following the throwing pattern outlined in the diagram. As they work on catching the ball with two hands, remind them to focus on quickly transferring the ball to their throwing hands, organizing their feet (toe-to-heel) and throwing. After two or three 30-second sessions of Hot Potato, have your players change from an overhand throw to a punch throw—a short, underhand toss without breaking the wrist. Emphasize the importance of these short throws and punches for middle infielders and development of quick ball exchange.

You can make this drill a competition by counting the number of throws made in 30 seconds by each group. The winning group is the group that makes the greatest number of successful throws.

Slow Rollers to Third Base D9

Purpose: To work on fielding ground balls hit slowly to third base, which includes charging to or through the ball, organizing the feet, and making an accurate throw to first base. (intermediate–advanced)

Have your players line up at third base, one behind the other. Hit, or throw by hand, slow rolling and slightly bouncing ground balls to third base. In turn, each player has a chance to field the ball. First have players charge the ball, quickly drop into a fielding stance, field the ball using two hands, organize the feet, and throw. After about three to five repetitions, or when they become comfortable with this play, players should practice charging *through* the ball as they bend on their glove-side leg to scoop the ball with the glove hand only. They should field the ball outside of their glove-side leg, and once it is in the glove, they use a toe-to-heel crow-hop, and throw the ball to first base. This drill can be performed at the same time as the Middle-Infield Double Play (see drill D10).

Middle-Infield Double Play D10

Purpose: To practice making the force-out at second base with an imaginary runner on first. This includes work on proper fielding, short throws and punch throws, and footwork around the base.

This drill works on getting the force-out at second base—including

Hot Potato

making short throws and flips and the proper footwork—between the short-stop and the second baseman. While either you or your assistant coach is hitting the ball for Slow Rollers to Third Base (see drill D9), the other coach stands on the second-base side of the pitcher's mound and rolls ground balls by hand to another group of players who take turns as the shortstop and second baseman. If the ball draws the fielder within 10 feet of second base, he uses a *punch* (a short, underhand toss without breaking the wrist) to throw to the second baseman. If the ground ball is more than 10 feet away from second base, the shortstop should make a short open step in order to organize the feet and make an accurate throw. The throw should be directed toward the middle of the baseman's chest. The receiver sprints toward the base, gathers himself for balance and places his throwing-side foot on the bag as he reaches toward the throw with the glove-side leg. The receiver holds up both hands, making a big and visible target for the fielder, and the catch is made using the two-hand technique.

Emphasize the importance of getting an out. Turning a double play at this level is extremely rare, whereas making an error in the attempt to do so is very common. Teach players to make the easy and routine play. This drill can be performed at the same time as the Slow Rollers to Third Base drill.

Turning Double Plays   D11

Purpose: To introduce fielders to turning a double play and to practice the necessary footwork and the precise timing, fielding, and throwing funda-mentals. (advanced)

This drill should be practiced by middle infielders only when they are very comfortable working together and have displayed proficiency in the Middle-Infield Double Play Drill (see drill D10). The drill is designed to make a force-out at second and get the batter-runner at first base. Primary focus is on proper footwork at second base. The key is for the fielder to stay out of the baseline as she attempts the throw to first base because that is where the runner will be.

If the second baseman is receiving the punch or overhand throw from the shortstop, he has a number of options. If he arrives at second base early, he can come across the base to the infield side of second, organize his feet out of the baseline and toward first, and make the throw. If he does not have time to come all the way across the base like this, he can receive the throw from the outfield side of second base with his glove-side foot on the base. He should show a target—both the glove and hand—to the shortstop. After making the catch with two hands, he pushes backward and out of the base-line onto his right leg and throws to first base. This is a long (60 feet) and difficult throw for the second baseman because his momentum is not going toward first, the runner is coming at him, and he must hurry. That is why making sure of the first out is so important to emphasize to your players.

If the shortstop is receiving the punch or overhand throw from the second baseman, she runs, or rather "glides," in a circle to the outfield side of second base and receives the throw while moving toward first base. It is important that the shortstop make a clear target with her glove and hands for the second baseman to see. As she catches the ball, she drops her right foot along the outside of the base, crow-hops toward first base while maintaining her momentum in that direction, and throws. The difficulty in making this play is the precise timing and the position of the throw that is necessary between the two infielders. Throwing to a moving target is much more difficult than throwing to a stationary one. Once again, many errors are made at this point, and the first out is lost. The advantage to this play, however, is that the shortstop has momentum toward first base, which shortens the distance of the throw.

This drill can be performed simultaneously with the Slow Rollers to Third Base (see drill D9). It requires many repetitions and precise teamwork, but it is a challenging and fun drill that kids really enjoy.

Ground Balls at Positions D12

Purpose: To work on fielding ground balls at players' respective positions and to work on making accurate throws to first base specific to each position. (easy–intermediate)

Diagram Key.
See also the field dimensions and positions diagram on page 15.

Players by position			
1	pitcher	**H**	home plate
2	catcher	**1**	1st base
3	1st baseman	**2**	2nd base
4	2nd baseman	**3**	3rd base
5	3rd baseman	→	run, sprint
6	shortstop	- - - -►	hit
7	left fielder	- - - -●	throw and catch
8	center fielder	**c**	coach
9	right fielder	▲	cone
		▽	bucket

Players assume their positions in the infield. If there is more than one player at a particular position, players should take turns receiving ground balls. Emphasize proper fielding techniques and accurate throws.

Begin by hitting short fungoes to your infield players from a 40- to 50-foot distance. This slower hit ball will help reduce their potential fear of being hit by the ball, and it also allows them to focus on the fundamentals of fielding the ball and making accurate throws. Hit balls in order from third base, shortstop, second base, and first base.

Once the infielders become comfortable with the short ground balls, move back to home plate and hit from there. Emphasize that this is like the real game and that they have worked hard to get to this point. This will challenge the fielder and increase his intensity.

If you have more than one first baseman, make sure that the players are alternating turns receiving throws, backing up the throw, and throwing in to the catcher working with you at home plate. Every once in a while, work on fielding bunts.

Bobbled Ball Drill D13

Purpose: To work on properly picking up a ground ball that has been bobbled and making an accurate throw.

One at a time, and at their respective positions, players drop a ball in front of themselves. Using quick footwork to get over and on top of the ball, they pick it up *with the throwing hand* but also get the glove down. They then quickly organize their feet using a toe-to-heel hop and throw to first base.

Dive Drill D14

Purpose: To practice getting up quickly after a diving stop to either the forehand or backhand and making an accurate throw.

One at a time, and at their respective positions, players start in a kneeling position facing home plate and with the ball in their gloves.

For a dive to the *forehand*, each player dives flat out to the forehand (glove-hand) side. He then scrambles to his feet, pushing up with both hands and feet, jumps into the toe-to-heel throwing position (this provides necessary momentum for the throw), and throws to first base.

For a dive to the *backhand*, each player dives flat out to the backhand (throwing-hand) side, scrambles to their feet, crow-hops gathering momentum toward first base, and throws.

Outfield

Wave Drill without Ball D15

Purpose: To work on the fundamentals of making outfield catches including first step, footwork, angle to the ball, use of two hands, and the crow-hop. This drill simulates several different types of catches, and by using no ball, you can more easily focus on the basics of breaks, angles, and running form.

Standing in front of a group in line facing you, point in the direction of a fly ball. Players break and sprint toward the imaginary fly ball. The different directions and angles include

1. 90 degrees to the left and to the right
2. 45-degree angle back—to the left and right
3. Directly over the head (point up and straight back)
4. In front of the fielder (point down at the ground)

For set 1, players pivot, sprint four or five strides 90 degrees to the left or right, set their feet under the fly ball, imitate the catch using two hands, crow-hop, and imitate the throw.

For set 2, players drop step their left foot as if the ball is over their shoulders to the left, or drop step open their right foot if the ball is to the right. They then sprint and make either the forehand or backhand catch (using the glove hand only) on the run, stop, crow-hop, and throw.

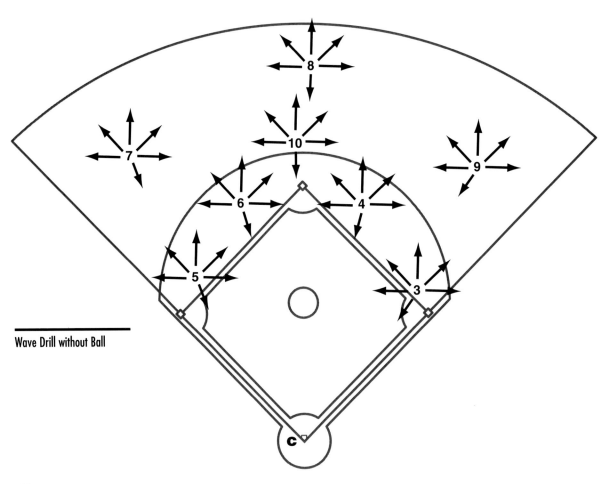

Wave Drill without Ball

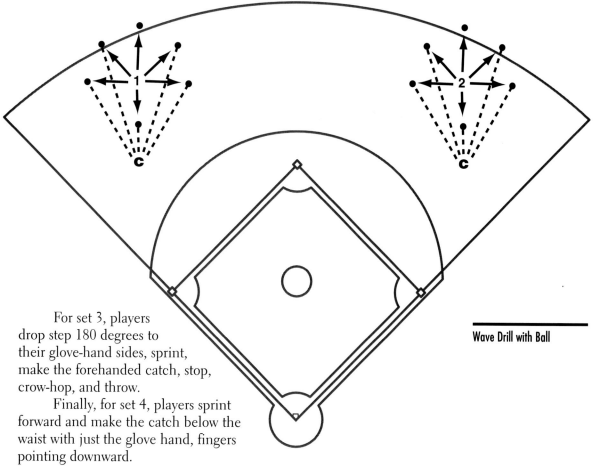

Wave Drill with Ball

For set 3, players drop step 180 degrees to their glove-hand sides, sprint, make the forehanded catch, stop, crow-hop, and throw.

Finally, for set 4, players sprint forward and make the catch below the waist with just the glove hand, fingers pointing downward.

Do two or three repetitions in each direction, focusing each time on a different aspect of the play, such as first step reaction, footwork, and proper angle. Run with the glove down with a natural arm swing until the player is ready to catch the ball. Most young players run with the glove hand out and up. This really decreases their running speed.

Wave Drill with Ball D16

Purpose: To continue work on the fundamentals of making stationary and running catches. Incorporating a ball into the drill leads one step closer to simulating game situations. (easy–intermediate)

Using a ball means that not all fielders can work at once. While infielders are working on ground balls (see drill D1), both you and the assistant coach can work with two lines of outfielders. The different types of catches follow the same order as the Wave Drill without Ball (see drill D15).

Have the player face you. Point 90 degrees to your left, and as soon as he begins sprinting, throw a fly ball in that direction. The player makes the catch, turns, crow-hops, and throws the ball back to the thrower.

The next player jumps in and goes through the same routine. Repeat the same procedure for each type of catch (over the left shoulder, over the right shoulder, over the head, and in front).

Give two repetitions for each player in each direction. Remember to allow the fielders time to settle underneath fly balls thrown at 90-degree angles. The rest of the fly balls, outlined in the Wave Drill without Ball, should be made as running catches. Players must jump in and out of the drill in order to keep it moving quickly—this should take only 7 to 8 minutes to get 5 or 6 repetitions for each player.

Quarterback Drill D17

Purpose: To work on making all-out running catches on balls thrown over the head. (intermediate)

Have your players line up in the outfield, one after another. Stand facing them in the infield. At your signal, the first player runs toward you, and you fake a hand-off as in a play-action pass. The player then sprints away from you, and you loft a fly ball high and over her throwing-side shoulder. She catches the ball and runs to the end of the line. Repeat this drill with the other players. When you get through the whole line, go to where the players are and run the drill back again. Give each player 5 or 6 repetitions in each direction.

Quarterback Drill

Outfielder's Ground Ball Techniques (without Ball) D18

Purpose: To work on three different techniques of fielding ground balls hit to the outfield. Fundamentals practiced in this drill include footwork, fielding position, and executing the crow-hop.

This drill is similar to the Wave Drill without Ball (see drill D15). Players spread out in the outfield and face you. As you call out "Block," "Infield position," or "Do or die," players respond with different fielding techniques.

- **Block technique:** fielders charge four or five steps forward, drop the knee of their throwing-hand side to the ground, and block and field the ball in front of the body.

- **Infielder's position technique:** fielders charge more aggressively and field the ball in an infielder's fielding position.

- **Do-or-die technique:** fielders charge the ball very aggressively and field the ball to the glove-hand side of the body. As the ball makes contact with the glove, players "give" with the baseball. Then they crow-hop and imitate the throwing motion.

Players perform two or three repetitions for each technique.

Outfielder's Ground Ball Techniques with Ball   D19

Purpose: To work on fielding ground balls hit to the outfield, including proper footwork, fielding position, and throwing motion. (easy–intermediate)

Players line up 80 to 90 feet away from you. Hit slow ground balls at them, drilling the block, infielder's technique, and do-or-die fielding techniques used in Outfielder's Ground Ball Techniques (without Ball) (see drill D18). Perform three to five repetitions for each technique and have outfielders return the balls by throwing them to a standing right beside you. Throws should be easy for the block and infield stance ground balls, but they should make game-like batted balls in the do-or-die portion of the drill.

Batted Fly Balls   D20

Purpose: To field fly balls and ground balls hit to the outfield. A major objective in this drill is to expose your outfielders to as many batted fly balls as possible so that they can develop the ability to judge a ball coming off of a bat. The drill also works on making accurate throws to a target. (intermediate)

Outfielders line up in centerfield. Hit fly balls to them from the right- or left-field line. Outfielders fielding a fly ball throw to a relay target, who then throws the ball back to your shagger. This will reduce the throwing distance for the outfielders and teach them to throw accurately to a target. Then have a player from the outfield replace the player who is the throwing relay target, who then goes to the end of the line in the outfield. After a number of fly ball repetitions, hit two or three rounds of ground balls.

The more skilled each player becomes at catching fly balls, the more difficult you can make the play. Focus primarily on getting into a proper fielding position, judging the fly balls, and catching with two hands above the face.

Communication Drill   D21

Purpose: To work on communication between outfielders on both fly balls and ground balls. Practicing this skill reduces the chance of players colliding in the outfield and provides realistic game experiences. (intermediate)

Stand on either the left- or right-field line and hit to the fielders in center field. Two outfielders spaced 40 to 50 feet apart are designated as the center fielder and right or left fielder. Throw or hit fly balls between the players and have them work on communication—calling "I've got it" or "You take it." Emphasize waiting to call for the ball until it reaches its apex and giving the center fielder priority in calling for the ball. This drill can also be done with outfield base hits, in which case the fielder who is called off backs up the fielder.

Team Defense

Relay Drill D22

Purpose: To practice making successful relays from the outfielder to the relay person and from the relay person to the base. The skills involved include crow-hops, receiving the throw, turning to the glove side, and throwing accurately.

Set up three complete groups of players and assemble them to make a relay line as shown in the diagram. Put infielders in the middle and outfielders and catchers at the ends. Each throw should be approximately 50 to 60 feet. Use one ball for each line of players. The ball is started at one end of each line, with the outfielder yelling, "Relay! Relay!" and is thrown to the infielder (middle), who waves his arms and yells, "Relay! Relay!" He should learn to adjust to off line throws, either running out to catch the ball in the air or running backward in order to catch it on one long hop. The infielder relays the ball to the other end of the line. This receiver throws it back to the infielder, who returns the ball to the starting point. Let each group complete 3 or 4 repetitions. Then these three players go to the end of their respective lines, and a new set of outfielders and infielders performs the relay drill.

Relay Drill

As your fielders develop this relay skill, emphasize catching the ball on the glove-hand side and with a turned body so that the process of turning and making the relay throw is quickened. This drill can be turned into a competition in which the first team to complete a set of four throws that end up back with the starting outfielder wins.

Comebacker Drill

Purpose: To teach pitchers to follow-through properly as they can field their position and defend themselves against batted balls hit right back at them.

Place a line of pitchers at the mound area. Hitting

fungoes, one or two hoppers, back at them, they feint a pitching motion follow-through and field the ball. The coach can have them throw to the first baseman for an out or to the shortstop for a force play. After fielding the ball, the pitcher should get his body and feet aligned to the target, crow-hop, and make a strong throw.

Bunt Rotation Drill   D23

Purpose: To practice the rotation of infielders and getting an out when a batter executes a sacrifice bunt with runners on base. (intermediate)

These simple rotations are designed to get the routine out at first base. Cutting down the lead runner is rarely an option if the bunt is laid down properly. The bunt rotations are determined by the following base runner situations:

Runner on first base: When the batter squares to bunt, both the first and third basemen charge to home plate. The second baseman rotates to first base and covers for the throw. The shortstop moves to cover second base in case there is a play to be made there. It is important that the catcher hustles to cover third base if the third baseman has fielded the bunt. This prevents the runner from going to third. This play must be drilled frequently.

Runners on first and second base, or just on second base: When the batter squares to bunt, the first baseman charges, but the third baseman holds her position at third. The pitcher is responsible for the third-base line, but if the ball is bunted past the pitcher, the third baseman must field the ball and throw to first base. Therefore, it is crucial that the pitcher and third baseman communicate—"I've got it," or "You take it." The second baseman rotates to cover first base, and the shortstop covers second. If the ball is fielded quickly, there is a chance of throwing the runner out at third base, but remember that it is only a force play if there is also a runner on first base. The rule of thumb is still to get the sure out, which is normally at first base.

Covering on a Steal   D24

Purpose: To practice what to do when a base runner steals a base, including who covers and who backs up the base. (intermediate)

With a runner on first base, make sure that the shortstop and second

Bunt Rotation Drill, runner on first base.

Bunt Rotation Drill, runners on first and second, or just second: Catcher covers third base if the third baseman has fielded the ball. If the pitcher or first baseman fields the bunt, the third baseman goes back to the base and the catcher stays at home.

Continued next page.

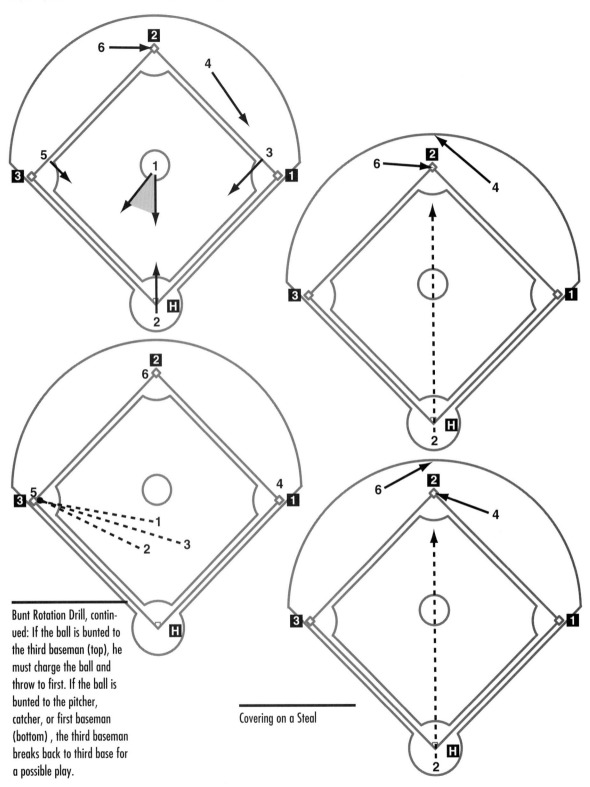

Bunt Rotation Drill, continued: If the ball is bunted to the third baseman (top), he must charge the ball and throw to first. If the ball is bunted to the pitcher, catcher, or first baseman (bottom) , the third baseman breaks back to third base for a possible play.

Covering on a Steal

baseman know who is covering second base in case the runner attempts to steal. If the batter at the plate is a strong hitter, players should anticipate that he will pull the ball. Thus, if the batter is right-handed, the shortstop holds her position, and the second baseman covers second base. If the batter is a lefty, the shortstop should cover the base. If the batter is not particularly strong, players should anticipate that he is less likely to pull the ball and should use the opposite coverage.

After the pitch, the cover man breaks to the base in case a steal is attempted, the fielder holding her position sprints behind second base in order to back up the throw from the catcher. The center fielder should also sprint toward the play as another backup if the ball is not batted.

If a player attempts to steal third base, the third baseman covers the base, and the left fielder sprints to back up the play.

Infield Practice   D25

Purpose: To practice making defensive plays common to players at each position, both infield and outfield, with the full defense on the field. (easy–intermediate)

This is also the same drill performed by the team before games as a defensive warm-up.

Infield Practice Setup (Pregame routine or practice). Infielders sequence: Coach fungoes one ground ball to each player at each position who throws to first base; do two rounds of this. For the older more skilled players, a round of double play balls should be hit. Lastly, bring the infield in. Fungo a soft ground ball and have infielders throw to the catcher for a tag play at home plate. Time: 7–8 min.

- **Play to second base:** This is the play when there is no runner on base or a runner on third base. For the left and center fielders, the shortstop is the relay man, and the second baseman covers second base. For the right fielder, the second baseman is the relay, and the shortstop covers second base.

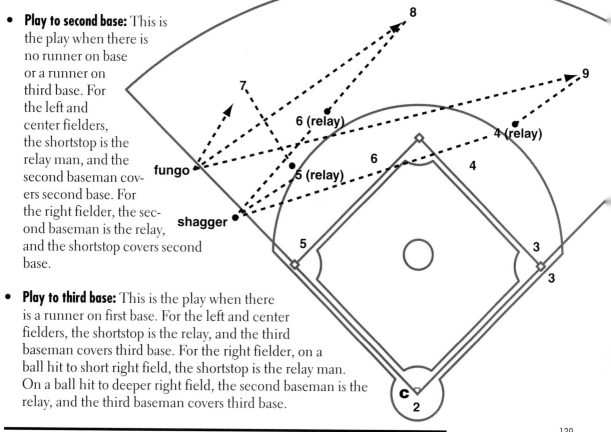

- **Play to third base:** This is the play when there is a runner on first base. For the left and center fielders, the shortstop is the relay, and the third baseman covers third base. For the right fielder, on a ball hit to short right field, the shortstop is the relay man. On a ball hit to deeper right field, the second baseman is the relay, and the third baseman covers third base.

- **Play to home plate:** This is the play when there is a runner on second base. For the left fielder, the third baseman is the cut-off man, and the catcher covers home. For the center and right fielders, the first baseman is the cut-off man, and the catcher covers home.

  Each outfielder gets one throw to each base. Then the outfield forms a line in center field, and the assistant coach hits fly balls to them one at a time.

- Ground balls to the infield—third base, shortstop, second base, first base. Throws to first base. 2 rounds.
- Ground balls to the infield. Third basemen throw to first, middle infielders make the force-out at second base, catcher fields a bunt and throws to first base.
- Ground balls to the infield. Outfielders are called in to the bench. All infielders are positioned on the infield grass, and throws are made directly to home plate for a tag or force play. After making each throw, infielders run in to the bench area.

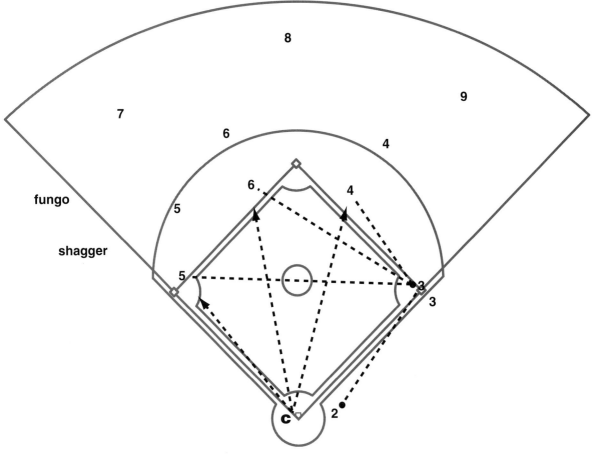

Batting Practice: Batting, and Playing Catcher

Batting

No-Bat Drill B1

Purpose: To teach the fundamentals of the swing without the distraction of actually holding a bat or hitting a ball. Fundamentals include stance, hands, launch position, stride, and swing.

Players assume the batting stance and look toward an imaginary pitcher. (They can focus on the batting practice pitcher if one is throwing.) As they get to the launch position, players check stride direction (toward the pitcher) and length (4 to 8 inches). Hands are at armpit level gripping the bat, the bat is tilted so the top hand is closer to the pitcher than the bottom hand, and there is firmness in the lead arm. The swing is initiated with a turn of the rear knee, hips and shoulders follow, hands are above the ball at contact, and in the follow-through phase the top hand rolls-over (rotates) the bottom hand. Eyes and shoulders remain level throughout. This drill can be performed in slow motion and at full speed. Each batter performs 10 to 15 swings.

Weighted Bat Drill B2

Purpose: To build wrist and arm strength while maintaining proper swing fundamentals. This drill also prepares the batter for the Dry Swings (see drill B3).

Each player uses a slightly weighted bat (2–3 oz. heavier) of some kind to perform this drill, which uses the same mechanics as in the No-Bat Drill (see drill B1). The drill is performed in slow motion. At the imaginary point of contact, the batter must hold the bat in a stationary position with the bat and hands level. After two seconds, the batter then continues the swing by rolling the top hand over and following through. Each batter performs 8 to 10 repetitions.

Dry swings. Work on visualizing different pitches and practicing good swing mechanics without the distraction of a ball.

outside
middle
inside
H
feet

Dry Swings B3

Purpose: To make fundamentally correct swings at pitches that are pictured mentally.

Immediately following the Weighted Bat Drill (see drill B2) the bat will feel much lighter to players, and swinging now at full speed seems easy. Each player should picture and swing at 4 or 5 pitches to four different locations: outside, inside, and high and low. The key to hitting pitches in these different locations is meeting the ball at the appropriate spot relative to the plate. The diagram shows that an outside pitch should be met toward the back of the plate, an inside pitch out in front of the plate, and a pitch down the middle at the front of the plate. Thus, the hands are in front of the head of the bat when hitting an outside pitch, behind the head of the bat when hitting an inside pitch, and even with the head of the bat when hitting a pitch in the middle of the plate. You can see, then, why a batter has less time to hit an inside pitch than an outside pitch. The point of contact is closer to the pitcher with an inside pitch, and so the ball takes less time to get there. Other than these adjustments, *the mechanics of each swing does not change.* Each batter takes a total of 12 to 15 swings.

The Tee-Hitting drill. Make contact with the ball at the front edge of home plate.

Tee-Hitting B4

Purpose: To practice hitting stationary baseballs set on batting tees.

Working in pairs, with one batter and one feeder (a partner who places the ball on the tee), players swing at stationary balls set on batting tees in the three different locations outlined in the Dry Swings drill (see drill B3)— outside, inside, and the middle of the plate. Players take 4 or 5 swings at each location then partners rotate. Batters need to take time to set up for each swing and to avoid rushing through the drill. Work on developing a good rhythm and good swing speed.

Soft Toss B5

Purpose: To practice hitting a moving baseball that can be tossed in any different pitch location. (easy–intermediate)

The batter hits into a net, a hanging rug, a screen, or a fence without pipes. The feeder (the partner tossing the ball) is approximately 12 to 15 feet away from the plate, out in front of the batter and at a more than 45-degree angle. The feeder shows the batter the ball and tosses underhand strikes to him in different locations. If the batter displays proficiency in hitting balls that are offered in the middle of the plate, the feeder can then begin working the outside and inside locations as well as high and low pitches as outlined in the Dry Swings drill. The diagram shows the location of these tosses relative to the plate. Feeders should work one location at a time for several repetitions before moving to another location. This gives the batter a chance to really work at a specific area. Fastballs can also be simulated. A toss that comes in on a line simulates a fastball and forces the batter to become quicker. Make sure that batters do not resort to bad habits, such as making an uppercut swing. Concentrating on and practicing proper fundamentals is the key to all of these drills.

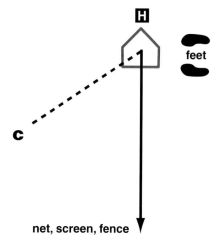

Batters will not always make it through all of these soft-toss stages and should not continue to hit if they become too tired. Players should get between 20 and 40 swings during these batting drills, however, before moving to Live Hitting (see drill B6).

> The Soft Toss develops proper swing mechanics, hand-eye coordination, and aggressive batting attitude.

Live Hitting B6

Purpose: To implement the proper batting fundamentals against live pitching. Batters also learn to be selective of pitches but be very aggressive on good pitches to hit. (intermediate)

The final stage in the hitting stations, this station should not be reached without mastering at least Dry Swings (see drill B3) and Tee-Hitting (see drill B4). Batters take 8 to 10 swings apiece. They are encouraged to swing only at strikes and not to let strikes go by without swinging. For players who struggle making contact with the ball, move the pitcher closer to the batter. However, make sure that you have a pitching screen to protect the pitcher, especially if a player is throwing the batting practice, rather than a coach. Those playing the field during live hitting need to play their positions and should treat the balls coming off the bat like game situations.

Bunt-in-a-Bucket B7

Purpose: To work on sacrifice bunting. The game rewards those who lay down accurate bunts on the third- and first-base lines.

In order to create pressure in a fun environment, a group of players (infielders or outfielders) lines up at home plate, and you or your assistant pitch. Set up two buckets, one on the grass just inside the third-base line and one on the opposite first-base line, and each 15 feet from home plate. Each player is thrown 6 strikes. The player tries to bunt the first three into the third-base bucket and the second three into the first-base bucket. The player with the most bunts in the buckets wins. If the bucket proves to be too small a target for your players, lay out a 4-foot 2 by 4 or 4-foot rope on both baselines instead of buckets.

Bunt-in-a-Bucket develops bunting accuracy toward both the first- and third-base lines.

Pitching and Catching

Fives Drill B8

Purpose: To work on the mechanics of the pitching motion. Accuracy is given significant priority over power in this drill, which also gives catchers, adorned in full equipment, much catching and blocking work.

Pitcher and catcher are 35 feet apart. The pitcher throws five pitches to four different locations—both corners and low and high in the strike zone. Proper mechanics and control are the primary areas of focus. The pitcher says "fastball low outside." He's calling his shot and this will help him to focus on specific locations.

- **Cocked position.** Place the pitcher in a stationary cocked position with the ball in his hand and his feet spread to a medium stride position. After you critique his position and technique, he throws 8 to 10 pitches at half speed at approximately 30 feet using proper trunk and shoulder rotation and follow-through. He should work on grooving the ¾ overhand motion.

- **Balance point.** The pitcher goes through her full pitching motion, but at the posting position she must remain balanced and closed on the pivot leg for 2 or 3 seconds. Do not throw. This drill teaches balance and proper alignment of the hips and shoulders to the plate.

- **Full motion.** This final stage allows the pitcher to go through the entire pitching motion without stops. Emphasize proper arm action and throwing in a good ¾ downward plane.

Catchers also get good work receiving a lot of pitched balls while wearing the mask and equipment. They should work on their own techniques of glove action and footwork.

Blocking the Ball Drill B9

Purpose: To give catchers practice at blocking balls thrown in the dirt.

A catcher's objective is not to catch the ball in the dirt. Rather, he wants to block it and keep it in front of him. In this drill, catchers start in the ready position—toes and heels on the ground, buttocks slightly raised, back bent, and glove up, making a target. From 10 to 15 feet away a partner throws Incredi-balls in the dirt to the catcher's right, to the left, and directly at him. The catcher moves laterally and forward to block the balls thrown to his right and left. As he moves to block, he slides to his knees, straightens his back, and blocks the hole between his legs with the mitt. For balls thrown in the dirt directly at him, he slides forward, goes immediately to his knees, and assumes the same blocking position. Performing 2 sets of 8 to 10 repetitions is a good workout.

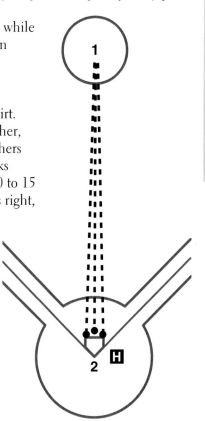

Fives Drill develops pitching accuracy and proper throwing mechanics. Gives catchers added work at receiving pitches.

Ending Activity: Scrimmage Situations

Situations Off Fungo Hits E1

Purpose: To create game situations to which your defense, fully assembled on the field, must react. It is also important to teach proper base-running reactions.

Set up a full defense in the field and a team of base runners, including batter-runners at home plate. As you hit balls to the defense simulating a batted ball in the game, the runners run the bases. By calling out the situation before hitting the fungo, you can create any game situation that you want to work on, from basic ground balls and fly balls, to force-outs and double plays, to bunt coverage and outfield relays. Use the time to teach and review the play. Players love this drill because it is game-like and challenging.

If you've got a lot of time invested in practice, sometimes a full scrimmage is a great way to end a practice.

Soft-Toss Scrimmage E2

Purpose: This drill simulates a real game but involves many more swings in a shorter amount of time than if pitchers were throwing.

Separate your players into two teams. Some players may have to play catcher or pitcher for both teams, and you can play in order to stretch out the numbers. The game is played like any other, except that the pitcher soft-tosses the ball to the batters, who swing away. You will normally have time for two or three innings.

Full Scrimmage E3

Purpose: To play a game and give your defense and pitchers a chance to work in a real game situation.

This is a full-fledged game with pitching and catching. Having a full scrimmage works best if you have a lot of time in practice. Most often, Situations Off Fungo Hits or Soft-Toss Scrimmage make for a more efficient practice. If you are going to scrimmage, have the coach (or assistant) umpire from behind the mound.

Skills Competition   E4

Purpose: To practice developing skills in a fun and competitive way. The competition also gives players a goal to aim for throughout the season as they work on the fundamentals of the game.

You can set up various games testing different baseball skills, such as the ones suggested here.

Throwing accuracy. In this drill, use small groups of players at a time. Tape two squares onto a wall or backstop, one inside the other. The outer square is about the size of a youth player's strike zone, and the inner square is about a third its size. Set up three rubbers, one 30 feet away, one at 45 feet, and one at 60 feet. Each player is allowed three throws at the squares and can choose the rubber from which to throw. Hitting the inner square from 30 feet counts 3 points; hitting the outer square counts 1 point. Hitting the inner square from 45 feet equals 5 points; hitting the outer square equals 2 points. And hitting the inner square from 60 feet yields 7 points; hitting the outer square yields 3 points. You can have as many rounds as you want, or the top four point scorers can compete against one another. The player with the most points wins.

Ground ball and fly ball knockout. Hit ground balls to infielders and fly balls to out-fielders. An error earns a player disqualification from the rest of the contest. The game continues as the number of players dwindles, and the last player remaining without making an error is the winner.

Bunting proficiency. Arrange one bucket on the first-base line and a second bucket on the third-base line. Place the buckets on their sides with the opening facing home plate. Each player is thrown six pitches and tries to bunt the first three pitches into the third-base bucket and the second three pitches into the first-base bucket. Each ball in the bucket is worth one point. The player with the most points wins.

APPENDIX: Umpire Signals

UMPIRE'S SIGNALS:

A. Right arm straight out front with palm outward and fingers up—signifies do not pitch, the ball is dead. **B.** Index finger of right hand is held above the head—signifies infield fly. **C.** Beckoning motion with right hand at head level while facing pitcher—signifies play is to start or be resumed and simultaneously umpire calls "Play." **D.** Left fist extended to the side at shoulder height—signifies an infraction for which (1) the penalty may be ignored or (2) bases may be awarded after no further advance is possible. Examples are: (a) catcher obstruction or umpire interference and (b) fielder's illegal use of equipment in checking a ball and obstruction by a fielder. **E.** Both hands open above the head—signifies time-out or ball is dead immmediately. **F.** Out—right hand extends out as if to shake hands and continues upward to right angle with closed fist slightly forward from the body. Coordinate verbal call, "He's out!", with the hammering action of the closed fist. **G.** Strike—fist up and then out away from body. **H.** Fair ball—point toward fair ground with open hand. **I.** Foul tip—the palms of the hands glance off each other as they pass above eye level. **J.** Foul ball—hands above the head, then with both hands motion to foul territory. **K.** Safe—hands should rise and extend in front of the body to shoulder height. Arms will then move in front of the body to each side of the body in continuous motion. Coordinate verbal call, "Safe," with outward extension of the arms. **L.** Place two fingers of the right hand on the left wrist, as if on top of a watch. This signal will only be used in two-out situations where a time play involving a potential run is likely.

A. Do not pitch, the ball is dead

B. Infield fly

C. Play

D. Delayed dead ball as for catcher obstruction

E. Time-out or ball dead immmediately as for a balk or batter being hit by pitch

F. Out

G. Strike

H. Fair Ball

I. Foul Tip

J. Foul Ball

K. Runner is safe

L. Time Play

Illustration courtesy National Federation of State High School Associations

Sample Scorebook

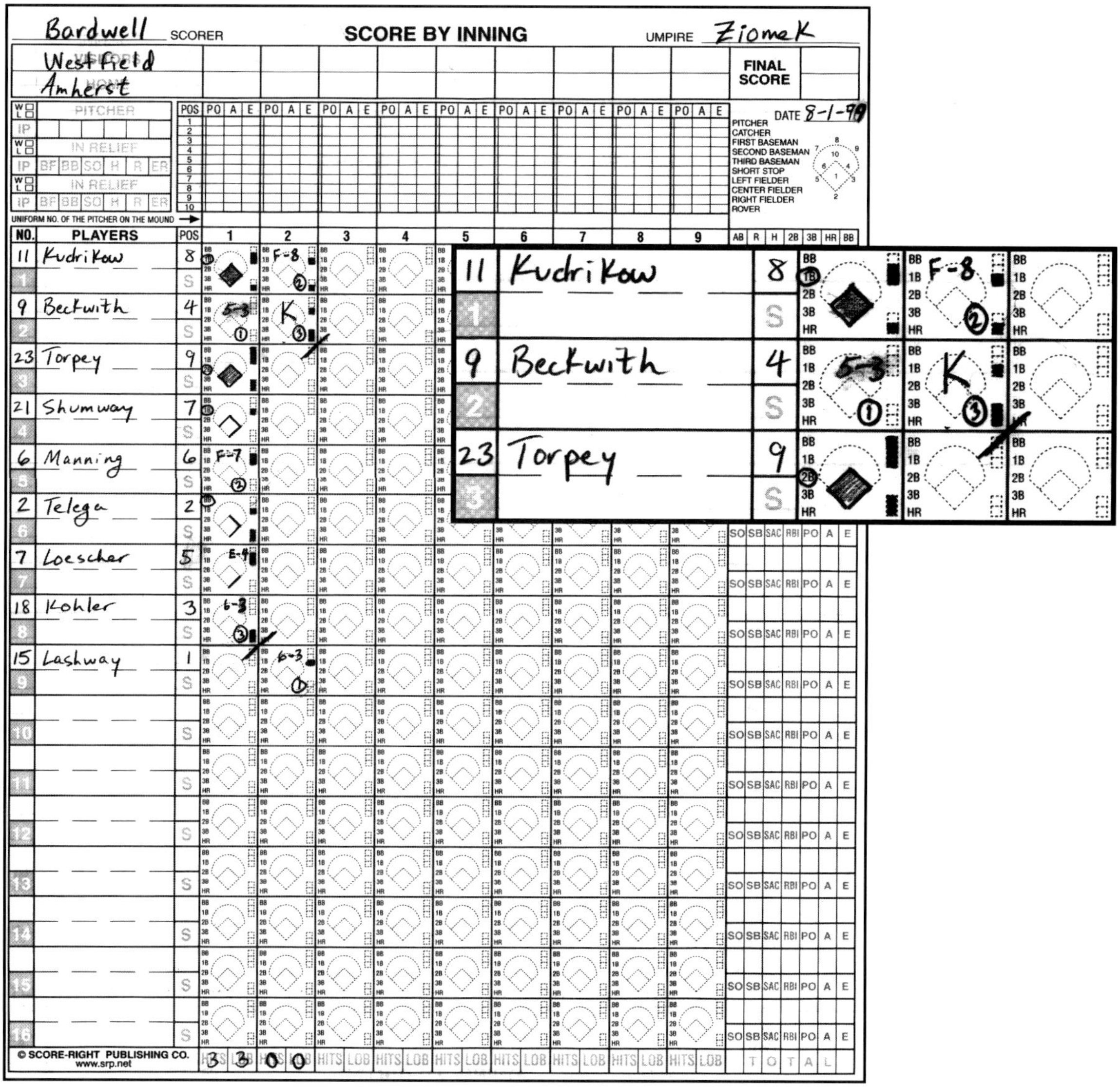

Glossary

Arm action: The movement of the throwing arm after the hands break in a throwing or pitching motion.

At bat: [statistic] A batting sequence in which a batter either makes an out, gets a hit, or reaches base on an error. Being hit by a pitch, a base-on-balls, and a sacrifice are not recorded as official "at bats."

Athletic stance: A balanced and ready position.

Attack the ball: While batting, taking an aggressive swing; while fielding, charging the ball aggressively.

Backhand: A catch made to the far throwing-hand side of the body with the glove positioned so that the fingers are above the thumb.

Backstop: A permanent protective screen behind home plate.

Bag: See *base*.

Ball: A pitch thrown out of the strike zone at which the batter does not swing.

Base: Four successive points at the corners of the infield that must be touched by a runner in order to progress to the next and score a run (first, second, third, and home). See also *home plate*.

Base coach: A team member or coach stationed in the coach's box at first or third base.

Base hit: Any hit ball that results in the batter safely reaching base without an error or a fielder's choice being made on the play.

Baselines: The two lines that run from home plate through first and third base, respectively. They separate fair territory from foul and extend beyond the bases to become the right and left field lines, respectively.

Base on balls: An award of first base granted to the batter who, during the time at bat, receives four pitches outside the strike zone. Also called a *walk*.

Base path: The running lane for base runners.

Base runner: An offensive player who is on base.

Bases loaded: The situation when base runners occupy first, second, and third base.

Batter: The player at bat.

Batter's box: A 4- by 6-foot area on the right and left sides of home plate in which the batter must stand when he is at bat.

Batting average: [statistic] The number of hits divided by the number of official at bats.

Bent-leg slide: A base-sliding technnique in which the bottom leg is flexed under the top leg, which extends to the base.

Block technique: The act of a catcher stopping an errant pitch with a mitt or leg.

Bottom of the inning: See *inning*.

Bunt: An intentionally soft hit made by the batter.

Catcher: Position 2, the fielder positioned behind home plate and primarily responsible for receiving pitches.

Center fielder: Position 8, the player positioned in the middle of the outfield.

Closed substitution: A rule that stipulates that a player cannot reenter a game after leaving.

Coach's box: A designated area adjacent to the bases along the first and third baselines from which a coach can direct runners and signal batters.

Cocked position: When throwing a ball, this is the position reached as the stride foot lands and just before rotation and arm acceleration occur.

Count: The number of balls and strikes thrown to a batter. The umpire acknowledges balls first and strikes second.

Covering the base: A reference to what a player does when responsible for plays at a given base.

Crow-hop: The technique used by players to organize their feet and gain momentum and power for making a throw.

Curve ball: A pitch that has an overspin and breaks sideward and downward. Not recommended for younger players to throw.

Cutoff: See *relay*.

Cut-off man: A defensive player positioned in the infield to receive throws directed to a base.

Do-or-die play: A fast, aggressive approach to a batted ground ball. The fielder plays the ball on the side witih the glove hand only.

Double: A two-base hit.

Double play: A play in which two outs are recorded on one batted ball.

Down the line: A reference to a batted ball hit near a foul line.

Drag bunt: A bunt that is pulled to the batter's side, for example, a left-handed batter bunts to the first-base side of the infield.

Earned run average: [statistic] The number of earned runs allowed by a pitcher divided by the number of innings pitched; the product of which is multiplied by the number of innings in a game (six at the youth level).

Error: A misplay made by a defensive player resulting in a runner or runners advancing to bases that they otherwise would not have reached.

Extra innings: Innings played beyond the normal stopping point (the sixth inning in youth league baseball) as a result of a tied score.

Fair ball: A legally batted ball that settles on or over fair territory.

Fair territory: All area inside and including the baselines.

Fastball: A high-velocity pitch thrown with backspin.

Fielder's choice: A defensive play in which the batter reaches base as a result of a defensive player opting to make a play on another base runner.

Fielding percentage: [statistic] The number of plays, putouts or assists, handled properly by a defensive player divided by the total number of chances.

First baseman: Position 3, the infielder responsible for plays at first base.

Fly ball: A ball hit in the air to the outfield.

Fly out: A ball caught by a defensive player before it touches the ground.

Follow-through: A term used in both throwing and batting to indicate the part of the throwing motion that occurs after the ball is released, or the part of the swing that occurs after the bat has gone through the contact area.

Force-out: An out made by tagging a base before it is reached by a runner required to move ahead by the runner behind her.

Force play: A play in which a runner legally loses the right to occupy a base by reason of the batter becoming a runner.

Forehand: A catch made to the far glove-hand side of a player with the glove positioned so fingers are below the thumb.

Form running: Proper sprinting technique involving both arm and leg action.

Foul ball: A ball that is hit into and touches foul territory.

Foul poles: The two poles that extend vertically at the points where the right and left field lines meet the outfield fence. A ball that hits a foul pole is considered to be "fair."

Foul territory: All area located outside the foul lines.

Free substitution: A rule permitting players to leave a game and reenter later.

Full count: Three balls and two strikes.

Fungo: A ball hit for practice fielding by a coach or player who tosses it into the air and hits it.

Fungo bat: A light, thin bat used by coaches in practice situations to hit ground and fly balls.

Grand slam: A home run hit with the bases loaded, resulting in four runs.

Ground ball: A batted ball that rolls along the ground.

Grounder: See *ground ball.*

Ground out: A play in which a defensive player, usually an infielder, catches a ball from the ground and relays a throw that beats a runner to a base.

Handcuffed: To hit the ball well below the barrel of the bat (or "off the handle") as a result of being late in swinging at an inside pitch.

Hit: See *base hit.*

Hit-and-run: A planned offensive play in which a base runner steals and the batter attempts to hit the pitch on the ground behind the runner.

Hit for the cycle: When a player hits at least one of each of the following in a single game: single, double, triple, and home run.

Hitting zone: The area in which the batter swings and attempts to hit a pitch.

Home plate: A 17-inch wide, five-sided slab of whitened rubber at which the batter stands and which must be touched in order to score.

Home run: A four-base hit in which the batter scores a run and is credited with an RBI.

In the gap: The space between outfielders into which a batted ball is hit.

In the hole: A reference to the area between infielders into which a batted ball is hit.

Incredi-ball: A sponge-filled, softer, safer version of a baseball that is used for a variety of drills, particularly at the youth level.

Infielder: A defensive player who plays in the dirt area of the diamond.

Infield fly rule: A fair fly ball that can be caught by an infielder with ordinary effort, when first and second, or first, second, and third bases are occupied before two are out. The batter is automatically ruled out.

Infielder's stance: A balanced athletic position ready to field a batted ball.

Inning: A unit of play defined by two half innings, in each of which three outs are recorded. The *top of the inning* refers to the first half of the inning, during which the visiting team bats. The *bottom of the inning* refers to the second half of the inning, during which the home team bats. A youth league game is usually composed of six innings.

Inside pitch: A pitch thrown anywhere between the middle of the plate and the batter's body.

K: See *strikeout*.

Launch position: The position reached during the batter's swing as the stride foot lands and just before the bat is accelerated forward toward the pitch.

Left fielder: Position 7, the outfielder covering an area behind third base.

Line drive: A hard hit batted ball that goes a distance on a horizontal plane.

Mitt: A catcher's or first baseman's glove.

On deck: The position of the next offensive player to bat.

On-deck circle: The area in which the on-deck batter warms up.

Out: A play in which a batter or runner is prevented from reaching a base. Three outs constitute one half inning.

Outfielder: A defensive player who is positioned beyond the infield dirt. The three outfield positions are left field, center field, and right field.

Outside pitch: A pitch thrown anywhere from the middle of the plate away from the batter's position.

Passed ball: A pitch that gets past the catcher and is ruled the fault of the catcher.

Pinch hitter: A substitute player who bats for the player listed in the lineup.

Pinch runner: A substitute player who runs for a player who has reached base.

Pitcher: Position 1, the fielder designated to deliver the pitch to the batter.

Pitcher's mound: The circular area, usually elevated, from which the pitcher throws to the batter.

Pitcher's rubber: See *rubber*.

Pocket of the glove: The inner portion of a baseball glove.

Pop fly: A fly ball hit high and short over the infield or short outfield.

Pop-up: See *pop fly*.

Punch throw: An underhand toss used at short range, usually between a shortstop and second baseman.

RBI: See *runs batted in*.

Relay: A defensive play in which an outfielder throws the ball to an infielder who, in turn, throws the ball to a teammate covering a base.

Relief pitcher: A player who enters the game to replace the current pitcher.

Right fielder: Position 9, the outfielder covering an area behind first base.

Rip: A hard hit ball.

Rubber: A rectangular whitened rubber slab set in the ground from which the pitcher must be in contact at the start of the motion. The distance from the rubber to home plate on a youth league field is 45 feet, and on a full size field it is 60 feet, 6 inches.

Run: A score awarded to the offensive team when a runner legally advances to home plate.

Runs batted in (RBI): [statistic] Credited to a batter when a runner scores because of the batter's action (there are a few exceptions to this).

Sacrifice bunt: A bunt in which the batter intentionally gives himself up in order to advance a runner to scoring position.

Sacrifice fly: A batted fly ball that is caught for an out but allows a runner at third base to tag up and score.

Safe: Arriving at a base before the defensive player's throw or tag.

Scoring position: A base runner on second or third base.

Second baseman: Position 4, the infielder positioned to the right of the second base bag.

Shortstop: Position 6, the infielder positioned between second and third base.

Sidearm: A throw in which the ball is released with the throwing arm near perpendicular to the body and horizontal to the ground.

Single: A one-base hit.

Slide: A baserunning technique in which a runner seeks to avoid a tag by dropping to the field and sliding. See *bent-leg slide*.

Soft hands: Catching the ball while gently bringing it to the body, as opposed to stabbing at it.

Stealing: In youth league, the act of advancing one base after the pitch has crossed the plate and was not hit by the batter.

Stirrups: The unique piece of a baseball uniform worn as an extra stocking over a player's inner hose.

Strike: Either a pitch that is entered in the strike zone but not swung at or a pitch at which the batter swings and misses or fouls off.

Strike zone: When the batter assumes her natural stance, the area over home plate from the bottom of the kneecaps to directly below the batter's armpits.

Strikeout: An out that is the result of three strikes being called, or when a batter swings and missed the third strike. Also called a *K* by the scorer.

Tag out: The act of a fielder tagging a base runner or a base with the ball securely in the hand or glove.

Tag up: A base runner returns to touch a base after a catch.

Take: The batter does not swing at a pitch.

Texas leaguer or Flare: A poorly hit fly ball that lands out of reach of a fielder. These hits are often called *flares* or *bloop hits*.

Third baseman: Position 5, the infielder positioned near the third-base bag.

Three-quarter overhead motion: The thrower's arm path comes forward and downward at approximately a 45-degree angle.

Toe-to-heel crow-hop: The technique used by infielders to gain momentum and quickly get their feet into a good throwing position after fielding a ground ball.

Top of the inning: See *inning*.

Triple: A three-base hit.

Triple play: A play in which three outs are recorded on one batted ball.

Umpire: The ruling official in a baseball game.

Uppercut swing: During the early phase of the batter's swing, the head of the bat drops too low and the path of the bat comes upward during the contact phase of the swing.

Up the middle: The area between the shortstop and second baseman.

Walk: See *base on balls*.

Wild pitch: A pitch thrown beyond the catcher's reach.

Resources

Associations and Organizations

Alliance of Youth Sports Organizations (AOYSO)
P.O. Box 351
South Plainfield NJ 07080
E-mail: info@aoyso.com
AOYSO is comprised of local youth sports associations whose goal is to provide high-quality and safe sports programs for young people.

Baseball Parent
4437 Kingston Pike, #2204
Knoxville TN 37919-5226
423-523-1274
http://members.aol.com/baseparent/
Baseball Parent is an organization for parents and coaches of youth baseball players. Baseball Parent has both an off- and online newsletter, college recruiting service, and other links.

Home Field Advantages, Inc.
P.O. Box 1355
Alexandria VA 22313-1355
E-mail: psavary@bellatlantic.net
http://www.homefield.org
Home Field Advantages is a non-profit organization that offers grant monies to help fund the construction and renovation of youth sports fields and facilities.

Little League Baseball, Incorporated
Little League Baseball International Headquarters
P.O. Box 3485
Williamsport PA 17701

570-326-1921
http://www.littleleague.org
Little League Baseball was founded in 1939. Its mission is to "promote, develop, supervise, and voluntarily assist in all lawful ways, the interest of those who will participate in Little League Baseball."

National Youth Sports Coaches Association (NYSCA)
800-729-2057
E-mail: nysca@nays.org
http://www.nays.org/nysca.html
NYSCA trains volunteer coaches in all aspects of working with children and athletics. In addition, coaches receive continuing education and insurance coverage and subscribe to a coaching code of ethics.

National Youth Sports Officials Association (NYSOA)
800-729-2057
E-mail: officials@nays.org
http://www.nays.org/nysoa.html
NYSOA trains volunteer youth sports officials, providing them with information on the skills required, fundamentals of coaching, and common problems they may encounter.

National Youth Sports Safety Foundation (NYSSF)
http://www.nyssf.org/
NYSSF is a nonprofit educational organization whose goal is to reduce the risks of sports injury to young people.

North American Youth Sports Institute (NAYSI)

http://www.naysi.com/
NAYSI's website features information and resources to help teachers, coaches, and other youth leaders, including parents, interact more effectively with children around sports. It includes a resource section that lists books on sports and coaching, as well as two interactive sections that give a browser an opportunity to submit questions on fitness, recreation, and sports. The website's newsletter, Sport Scene, focuses on youth programs.

Parents Association for Youth Sports (PAYS)

http://www.nays.org/pays.html
PAYS provides materials and information for youth sports programs to help teach parents about their roles and responsibilities in children's sports activities.

START SMART Sports Development Program

800-729-2057, 561-684-1141
Fax 561-684-2546
E-mail: startsmart@nays.org
http://www.nays.org/startsmart.html
START SMART is designed to teach parents how to best help their children develop the motor skills necessary for a successful start in sports.

Websites and Electronic Newsletters

Adapted Physical Education

http://pe.central.vt.edu/
E-mail: pec@vt.edu
This section of PE Central (see below) offers information to help teachers of physically challenged students. The site suggests many ways to modify sports and activities to make them accessible to all students. In soccer, for example: substitute walking for running; have well-defined boundaries and reduced playing area; play six-a-side soccer; allow wheelchair-bound students to keep the ball on their laps; use a target that makes noise when hit; use a deflated, brightly colored, nerf, or beeper ball.

Baseball Coach's Corner

http://www.teamdiscovery.com/baseball/coach/
The Baseball Coach's Corner provides online advice and information about all aspects of coaching youth baseball, including a complete Coaching Library and Ask the Coach forum.

Coaching Youth Sports

http://www.chre.vt.edu/~/cys/
Virginia Tech's Health and Physical Education program sponsors this website, which provides coaches, athletes, and parents with general, rather than sport-specific, information about skills for youth. The site also allows browsers to submit questions.

John Skelton's Baseball Links

http://www.baseball-links.com
This site offers more than 5,000 links to baseball-related sites, including a state-by-state directory of youth baseball leagues.

Officiating.com

E-mail: Feedback@Officiating.com
http://www.officiating.com/
This website offers news, including updates on rule changes; coaching philosophy and mechanics; and discussion boards.

PE Central

http://pe.central.vt.edu/
This website for physical education teachers, students, and parents is designed to provide the most current information on appropriate physical education programs, helping young people on their way to a lifetime of physical fitness and health.

Sports Parents

http://www.sportsparents.com/
Sports Parents provides a variety of articles from the magazine Sports Parents, a supplement to Sports Illustrated for Kids. Topics include coaching, sportsmanship, nutrition and fitness, equipment, sports medicine and safety, and finance and travel. A parents' tips section covers issues such as winning and losing, sibling rivalry, helping a child cope with frustration, and self-esteem.

WebBall

E-mail: coach@webball.com
http://www.webball.com
WebBall offers dozens of baseball topics, including conditioning, nutrition, and first aid, that one can browse for one-page printable sheets of tips, drills, and strategies.

World of Sports: Youth Sports on the World Wide Web

http://www.worldofsports.com/
This website offers a coaches forum and an extensive list of links by subject matter to other relevant sites.

Youth Sports Network

http://www.ysn.com/
Youth Sports Network is a multifaceted site with a featured sport of the week, news stories about youth sports, and a directory of sports camps. An instructional page covering soccer, basketball, baseball, and softball offers tips and ideas for both players and coaches. The site also offers information on exercise, nutrition, and first aid.

Index

Numbers in **bold** refer to pages with illustrations. The glossary and resources have not been indexed.

A

ability
  disparities in, 13
  positioning by, 73
Above, below, and at Waist High drill, 81–82, 122–23
advanced practice, 90–93
alertness
  of bench players, 21, 102
  to health problems, 65
All-at-Shortstop drill, 83, 87, 108, 126–27
arm
  avoiding injury of, 23
  in pitching, 53
  in throwing, 38
Arm Swings drill, 81, 118
assistant coach, 27–28
athletic stance, **41**–42
attitude
  of pitcher, 18–19
  toward baseball, 105

B

backhand catch, 37, **43**
Backhand drill, 87, 123–24
balance point, of pitcher, 53, **54**, 144
ball, 16
  fair, 16
  fly. *See* fly balls
  foul, 16, 102
  ground. *See* ground balls
  passed, 17
  in play, 16–20
  See also baseball (ball)
Ball to Glove-Side drill, **82**, 123
Ball to Throwing-Side drill, **82**, 123
ballfield, **15**

base(s)
  positions at, 14, **15**
  sprinting to, 99
  ways to reach, 17
base hits, 17
base on balls (walk), 16
base runner, 17
  instructing during games, 106, 109–10
  outs by, 17
  in scoring position, 97, 104
  tagging and throwing out, 44–**45**
base running, 17, **64**–66
  aggressive, 99, 109–10
  drills, 65, 118–22
  form running, 64–65, 81, 86
  sliding, 23, 65–66, 121–22
  stealing, 17, 105, **137**–39
baseball (ball), 30
baseball (game)
  basic rules, 14–20
  field, **15**
  positions, 14, **15**
basic beginning practice, 81–85
bat, 29
  fungo, 75
  matching to batter, 29, 59
  weighted vs. "donut," 29
Batted Fly Balls drill, 88, 135
batter
  matching to bat, 29, 59
  outs by, 16
  positioning of, 19
  ways to reach base, 17
batter's box, 19
batting, 57–62, **60**, **61**
  bunting, 62–64, **63**, 103–4, 137, 144, 147
  in games, 103–4, 105–6, 109
  grip, **58**, 59, **60**
  order, in game, 100
  safety in, 22–23
  stance, **59**
  and take sign, 103, 105–6

batting practice, 74–75
  in advanced practice, 92
  in basic beginning practice, 83–85
  drills, 61, 141–45
  importance of, 23
  in intermediate practice, 88–89
  with large team, 32
  problems in, 93
bench players, 21, 101, 102
bent-leg slide, **66**
Bent-Leg Slide drill, 90, 121–22
block technique, **48**, 49, 134
Block Work drill, 85
Blocking the Ball drill, 145
Bobbled Ball drill, 87, 131
boys, coaching, 113, 115
"Bring it in!" command, 10, 12–13, 67–68
Bunt Rotation drill, 91, **137**, **138**
Bunt-in-a-Bucket drill, 91–92, **144**
bunting, 62–64, **63**
  drag, 64
  drills, 64, 91, **137**, **138**, 144, 147
  in games, 103–4
  for hit, 64, 104
  sacrifice, 62–**63**, 103–4

C

call to parents preseason, 25
calling the ball, 22, 48
catcher, 31, **56**–57
  conquering fear of ball, 58
  drills, 144–45
  equipment for, 30, 31
  positioning of, 14
  practicing playing, 85, 89, 92, 144–45
catching, 34–37, **35**
  in advanced practice, 90, 92
  in basic beginning practice, 81–82, 85
  by catcher, **56**–57, 144–45

Acknowledgments

The author would like to acknowledge the following people:

Tim Loescher, for his help in writing this book.

Ed Woodbury, my high school coach in Norway, Maine, who showed me the importance of proper fundamentals and instilled in me a love and respect for the game.

Ray Fisher, my college coach at the University of Michigan, who taught me the arts of throwing and pitching.

Chester Thurston, my father, who was a dairy farmer and instilled in us a solid work ethic and a philosophy of "whatever you do, be good at it."

About the Author

Coach Bill Thurston has been a long-term successful college baseball coach who is also nationally and internationally recognized as a teacher of proper baseball techniques and skills. In addition to speaking at more than two hundred clinics throughout the United States, he has coached and served as a clinician for national teams in Australia, Canada, China, the Netherlands, Italy, Panama, and Romania.

Coach Thurston has produced four videos on the various phases of pitching and throwing, written an instruction manual for pitchers and pitching coaches, and has served as Baseball Rules Editor for the NCAA for the past fifteen years.

Twenty of his Amherst College players have played professionally and two became major league pitchers. A number of former players have become college coaches; other former players have become coaches, scouts, and administrators in professional baseball.

Coach Thurston has been inducted into the American Baseball Coaches Association's Hall of Fame, has been selected the New England College Coach of the Year four times, and in 1997 was presented the Dr. James R. Andrews Award by the American Sports Medicine Institute for his research and contributions to sports medicine.

Coach Thurston grew up in Maine and received a baseball scholarship at the University of Michigan, where he was a pitcher and an outfielder. He played professionally in the Detroit Tigers organization. Over the past thirty-five years at Amherst College in Massachusetts, Coach Thurston's teams have won 70 percent of their games. He is currently the head baseball coach and a tenured professor of physical education.